EDUCATING STREET KIDS

Educating Street Kids

*A Ministry to Young People
in the Charism of Edmund Rice*

PAUL WILSON, C.F.C.

ALBA · HOUSE   NEW · YORK

SOCIETY OF ST. PAUL, 2187 VICTORY BLVD., STATEN ISLAND, NY 10314

Library of Congress Cataloging-in-Publication Data

Wilson, Paul R.
    Educating street kids: a ministry to young people in the charism of Edmund Rice / Paul Wilson.
       p. cm.
    Includes bibliographical references.
    ISBN: 0-8189-0659-6
    1. Church work with juvenile delinquents. 2. Juvenile delinquents — Education. 3. Homeless youth — Education. 4. Rice, Edmund Ignatius, 1762-1844 — Influence. 5. Christian Brothers — Missions. 6. Christian Brothers — Education. 7. Catholic Church — Education. 8. Covenant House — (New York, N.Y.) 9. Homeless youth — New York — Case studies. I. Title.
    BV4464.5.W53   1993
    259'.23 — dc20   93-6710
                                                                                   CIP

Produced and designed in the United States of America by the
Fathers and Brothers of the Society of St. Paul,
2187 Victory Boulevard, Staten Island, New York 10314,
as part of their communications apostolate.

ISBN: 0-8189-0659-6

Copyright 1991 by Paul Wilson, CFC

Printing Information:

Current Printing - first digit	1	2	3	4	5	6	7	8	9	10
Year of Current Printing - first year shown										
1993		1994		1995		1996		1997		1998

CONTENTS

Preface vii

Introduction ix

Biblical Abbreviations xii

Chapter 1:   Missiological Concerns 1

Chapter 2:   A Need In Our Times 9

Chapter 3:   Edmund Rice — Liberator 43

Chapter 4:   Edmund's Texts 53

Conclusions 85

The Centre Education Programme 89

A Discussion Guide 93

Bibliography 97

ACKNOWLEDGMENTS

Originally published by St. Paul Publications, Society of St. Paul. 60-70 Broughton Road, Homebush, NSW, Australia under the title: *A Mission of Justice: Refounding a ministry to young people in the charism of Edmund Rice*, © 1991 by Paul Wilson, CFC.

Extracts from *A Spiritual Profile of Edmund Ignatius Rice, Vol. I, More Than Silver Or Gold*, 1984, and *A Spiritual Profile of Edmund Ignatius Rice, Vol. II, Rooted In Love*, 1985 by A.L. O'Toole, used by permission of Congregation of Christian Brothers, English Province, Liverpool, England.

Extracts from *Edmund Rice: The Man and His Times*, by D. Rushe, 1981, and *Edmund Ignatius Rice and the Christian Brothers*, by W.M. McCarthy, 1926, used by permission of Gill and Macmillan, Dublin, Ireland.

Extracts from *The Gospel of Peace and Justice*, edited by J. Gremillion, 1971, used by permission of Orbis Books, New York, USA.

Extracts from *The New American Poverty*, by Michael Harrington, 1984, used by permission of Henry Holt and Co., Inc., New York, USA.

Extracts from the book, *The Moral Life of Children*, by Robert Coles, copyright © 1986 by Robert Coles. Published by The Atlantic Monthly Press, New York, USA and used by permission.

Extracts reprinted by permission of Greenwood Publishing Group, Inc., Westport, CT, USA from *A Pedagogy for Liberation* by Shor and Freire, 1987.

PREFACE

This study arose from questions some Christian Brothers were asking about how the followers of Edmund Rice might meet the challenge today to "make an option for the poor" — to practice their educational ministry among the poorest of youth.

Teaching religious and their co-workers are experts at classroom tasks, school administration and pastoral care of children and youth. Some have even ventured into the world of the streets and the truants who inhabit them. But others are afraid and, while admiring the pioneers, have little understanding of, or confidence in, making a radical departure from their traditional ministries in the schools. Yet the world and the Church are pointing clearly to the educational needs of these "new urban poor," and some in the Church feel an accusing finger pointing at them.

The experiences of Paul and myself, and shared by some with whom we worked, led us to believe that the educational and theological foundations of what it meant to teach in a traditional school — to set up teaching strategies, to evangelize, to assess people intellectually and emotionally — were really culturally based related behaviors, and the world of the marginalized was in fact another culture. The poor people of Mount Druitt and Logan City, on the outskirts of Sydney and Brisbane, were often capable of faith responses they should not have achieved according to the "stage theory" norms of Kohlberg and Fowler. Sensitivity and depth of social analysis were evident in their conversations.

Reflecting academically on these unsettling experiences of trying to transplant traditional "education" across this gap, we turned to the disciplines of anthropology, sociology and contextualized theology to help us bring a cross-discipline frame of analysis to the situation.

The two of us set off with the same questions, taking the marginalized youth of New York City as our sub-culture to investigate. I examined the questions from the point of view of an "educator," using anthropological analysis, and Paul examined the world of these youth from the perspective of theology, using social analysis. The outcomes of our studies were submitted eventually as a Doctoral dissertation from Columbia University, and a Master's dissertation from Maryknoll School of Theology. This book is a result of Paul's Master's work with reference to my own field work and data.

Peter Hancock, CFC

INTRODUCTION

Whether they are referred to as *los niños trabajos* (as are the shoe-shine boys of Lima), or *tromposi* (the pickpockets of Sao Paulo, literally those who "hit against one"), or simply the "street kids" of Times Square, New York, the world's poor are increasingly homeless, unemployed, illiterate, colored and quite young. South American estimates suggest that by the year 2000, 80% of the population will be under 21. In 1988 the American Center for Children in Poverty rated its own under-six population as containing some 23% of the country's poor. Despite government family planning strategies, Asia and Africa provide similar statistics.

These young people have all the qualities of the so-called "urchins" of 18th and 19th-century English literature. They are often hungry, are forced to steal to survive and live quite alienated from mainstream society. Social activists condemned the practices which in Charles Dickens' days caused the phenomenon: the evils of factory owners and the attitudes of the emerging wealthy middle class. To date condemnation, even identification, of the modern causes of this widespread suffering is not so forthcoming.

Some in the Europe of the Industrial Revolution sought lasting remedies, usually by adjusting factory conditions or changing laws; a few tried social experiments. Education was not initially seen as a solution to the numbers of waifs. In Ireland, however, Edmund Rice, founder of the Christian Brothers, significantly altered the social expectations of generations of Irish young men through education.

The poverty of Ireland at the time was the result of its

domination by England, attributable particularly to the colonizing mentality bred by the Industrial Revolution. It was compounded by religious antipathy and institutionalized through a series of harsh government decrees that combined the causes of oppression into a single act of subjugation. The climate was one of economic hardship, religious intolerance and political suppression.

Following the death of his young wife in 1789, Edmund spent some 10 years discerning his future. Amidst a time of his own increasing wealth as a successful Waterford merchant and yet also a time of increasing prayer and Christian commitment, Edmund saw the plight of the poor youngsters of his neighborhood. In 1802 he was ready to devote his wealth to founding free schools for the poor, a work that was so successful it had spread to England and Australia before the end of the century and today is represented in Africa, the Americas and India as well. Crucial to this development was the motivation of empowering the poor through education.

In our age when the phenomenon of street youth is almost universal, Edmund Rice's vision could again be of great service to the world. The refounding of this ministry in new and creative ways in our times depends on an accurate appreciation of the dynamics of Edmund's original foundation. This is nothing less than the challenge offered the followers of Edmund Rice and those interested in this ministry by the Church in post-conciliar times: to align the signs of the times with the charism of Edmund Rice and ultimately with the Word of God in Scripture.

But the configuration of these factors for those in youth ministry today will be somewhat different from Edmund's. New times require new responses. The reading of history is validated by the freedom it gives for present actions. To be true to the original mission and to Scripture, a new configuration of the signs of the times, the charism of the founder and Scripture is required. This new shape will be found by re-reading history in the light of the present experiences to discover themes already occurring though not necessarily remembered. The present hermeneutical approaches to

Scripture offer a suitable model for this process of re-reading and will be applied here also to Edmund's biographies.

For religious congregations, ministry happens within the context of mission. The gospel task of evangelization as defined by the particular charism of the institute nurtures a particular ministry or even groups of ministries. It is evident then that a refoundation of a ministry to street kids will require a reformulation of an understanding of mission within the charism of Edmund Rice.

Therefore, this work commences with a review of present positions on mission; proceeds through an analysis of the social problem of street kids, including an educational model for action; offers a re-reading of Edmund Rice's life to determine his own understanding of mission; extends this through an exegesis of the scriptural texts he wrote during the time of his "conversion"; and concludes by proposing new forms of ministry and a renewed understanding of mission for the followers of Edmund Rice and others interested in this ministry.

It will be seen that, arising from the material under consideration, the question of justice is of paramount importance to the Christian Brothers and their co-workers as they seek to redefine their mission in these times and to refound the ministry Edmund bequeathed to the Church.

BIBLICAL ABBREVIATIONS

OLD TESTAMENT

Genesis	Gn	Nehemiah	Ne	Baruch	Ba
Exodus	Ex	Tobit	Tb	Ezekiel	Ezk
Leviticus	Lv	Judith	Jdt	Daniel	Dn
Numbers	Nb	Esther	Est	Hosea	Ho
Deuteronomy	Dt	1 Maccabees	1 M	Joel	Jl
Joshua	Jos	2 Maccabees	2 M	Amos	Am
Judges	Jg	Job	Jb	Obadiah	Ob
Ruth	Rt	Psalms	Ps	Jonah	Jon
1 Samuel	1 S	Proverbs	Pr	Micah	Mi
2 Samuel	2 S	Ecclesiastes	Ec	Nahum	Na
1 Kings	1 K	Song of Songs	Sg	Habakkuk	Hab
2 Kings	2 K	Wisdom	Ws	Zephaniah	Zp
1 Chronicles	1 Ch	Sirach	Si	Haggai	Hg
2 Chronicles	2 Ch	Isaiah	Is	Malachi	Ml
Ezra	Ezr	Jeremiah	Jr	Zechariah	Zc
		Lamentations	Lm		

NEW TESTAMENT

Matthew	Mt	Ephesians	Ep	Hebrews	Heb
Mark	Mk	Philippians	Ph	James	Jm
Luke	Lk	Colossians	Col	1 Peter	1 P
John	Jn	1 Thessalonians	1 Th	2 Peter	2 P
Acts	Ac	2 Thessalonians	2 Th	1 John	1 Jn
Romans	Rm	1 Timothy	1 Tm	2 John	2 Jn
1 Corinthians	1 Cor	2 Timothy	2 Tm	3 John	3 Jn
2 Corinthians	2 Cor	Titus	Tt	Jude	Jude
Galatians	Gal	Philemon	Phm	Revelation	Rv

CHAPTER ONE

MISSIOLOGICAL CONCERNS

The 1832 rule of the Christian Brothers stated the mission of the Congregation in the following terms:

> The Brothers should recollect that the instruction of poor children is the great object of their Institution, and for which, through the mercy of God, the Institute has been particularly raised up. They should always teach them gratis; nor can they receive from them or their parents, anything by way of retribution for their education; but shall content themselves with the glorious recompense promised to all who instruct many unto justice.[1]

This statement of the mission of the Congregation in the first rule of the Institute, written during the life of the founder, articulates well the attitude of the early Brothers and of Edmund Rice himself to ministry to the poor. It was seen as fulfilling the scriptural promises for those who *instruct many unto justice*. The object of the Institute, the instruction of the poor, is seen to be rewarded by God, as is all instruction "unto justice."

Given the import of the 1832 rule for the Congregation, this statement of mission must be seen as foundational for Edmund

---
[1] *Constitutions of the Christian Brothers*, 1985, p. 47.

Rice's followers. What was meant by using this biblical reference to "instruct many unto justice" is unclear solely from the context. It will be necessary to investigate the life of the founder and his own use of Scripture to clarify the meaning of the term.

By comparison with this early rule, the concept of mission in the 1985 constitutions is rather bland and unfocused. It details the specific task of the Brothers but without the underlying motivation seen in the 1832 rule.

> The specific mission entrusted to us by the Church is the evangelization of youth through the apostolate of Christian Education, and as religious Brothers in a Congregation of pontifical right, devoted to works of the apostolate, we move in response to the call of the Church and the needs of the times.[2]

Admittedly, the chapter on mission in these latest constitutions extends this thought to include both the element of service to the poor, "especially the education and care of the materially poor,"[3] and that of justice and the dignity of all persons: "We endeavor to proclaim gospel values, to affirm the dignity of all persons and to work for peace in a truly just society."[4]

What appears to be lacking here is the thrust offered by the motivation to "instruct many unto justice" that is given for mission in the statement of 1832. The ensuing study is made against the background of this statement with the hope that its meaning and import for the early Brothers and for the Congregation today may become clearer. It is expected that the relevance of the 1832 vision of mission for today's world and Church will become obvious.

---

[2] Ibid., p. 2.
[3] Ibid., p. 11.
[4] Ibid., p. 12.

Mission in Today's Church

Much has been written in recent years to redefine the mission of the Church in the world. Essentially, the positions could be reduced to two. On the one hand is the *spiritual mission* of the Church, what William Burrows calls "the instrument of grace" model, where the Church exists to communicate God's saving grace to humankind.[5] It has been from this model that the mission statements of the Christian Brothers in the past, including that of 1832, have been largely drawn since this was the prevailing theological thought. But now, as Burrows makes clear, this model has been seen as inadequate. More recently, the personal and otherworldly dimensions of salvation of this model are offset by a concept of the *temporal mission* of the Church in which the transformative and historical dimensions of salvation are emphasized as, for example, in the theologies of liberation.

Writing from this theological position, Dominique Barbe supplies one way of seeing the consistency between the former missiology with its emphasis on grace and the present missiology with its concern for transformation. He determines that the final objective of the Christian mission of the world is the realization of love. Barbe speaks of the Christian task as the installation of love on earth, preparatory to the completion of love in the final reign of God in eternity. He says that the world of solidarity can only be sketched in this present life but that the life of love must be commenced, at least, if the completion of God's reign is ever to occur.[6]

This is the essential mission of the Christian. It is the primary aim also, no doubt, of the instrument-of-grace model of mission. After all, the Gospel claims its center to be the twofold commandment: "You must love the Lord with all your heart, with all your soul

---

[5] William Burrows, *New Ministries: The Global Context* (Maryknoll: Orbis Books, 1980), p. 38.

[6] Dominique Barbe, *Grace and Power: Base Communities and Non-Violence in Brazil* (Maryknoll: Orbis, 1987), p. 26.

and with all your understanding... [and] you shall love your neighbor as yourself" (Mt 22:37, 39). The two models share this single injunction as their basic orientation. What differs in the transformative model is the emphasis given the horizontal dimension of the love command. Barbe asks how the Christian can speak of love in a *favela* trembling with cold and hunger if the houses about it are shrouded in warmth and comfort.[7]

It is this grounding of mission in the real conditions of today's world that is providing the tension within the Church between the two axes of the single commandment of love. Christians readily agree that their task is to love concretely, even perhaps to show a "preferential option for the poor" (CELAM Conference, Medellin, 1968), but the kind of love being spoken of by Barbe includes a dimension of justice and this is often rationalized away as "Old Testament thought." An instrument-of-grace model of mission can easily see justice as too political and this-worldly a concept for Christians.

As Burrows suggests, a new missionary formulation in the future will encompass both models.[8] As this is approached, the present task is to select from both models the elements which ensure that the Church is faithful at one and the same time to its essential character *and* to the needs of the world today. Within the Church, the followers of Edmund Rice are being challenged to reformulate the nature of their mission is these same terms.

A World in Need

Most of the world's people live in conditions that are less than comfortable, if not close to life-threatening. Whether in situations of hunger as in Somalia and the Sudan or of poverty as in much of

---
[7] Ibid., p. 26.
[8] William Burrows, *New Ministries*, 1980, p. 51.

Asia, Africa and South America or of institutionalized violence as under the repressive regime of South Africa during the years of apartheid, these conditions are far from the comprehension of most white, Western, First-World Christians. Ministry in this world must take the forms of compassion *and* justice.

There is sufficient evidence that the justice dimension of the new formulations of mission will be crucial to the efficacy of the Church in the coming generations. It is enough to look at the progression of Church documents relating to questions of justice in recent years. From Paul VI's *The Development of Peoples* (particularly Nos. 22 and 24) to the American Catholic Bishops' *Statement on the Economy*, the list of social justice statements continues to increase. Pope John Paul II has continued the trends of his predecessors in this regard (cf. *Laborem Exercens* and *Solicitudo Rei Socialis*).

One means of analyzing this trend of the Church towards a concentration on its mission of justice is to focus on the sociological patterns that predict future religious practice. Two excellent analyses have already emerged which define the future Church by its stance with the poor in justice and in solidarity.

In her comprehensive analysis of the conditions of the poor in the world today and their relation to theology, Marie Augusta Neal argues for a prophetic Church in our times. She suggests that an altruism that means a giving of oneself even to death will be the necessary sign of the disciple in the world. For such a value to become important, the consciousness of Christians for the conditions of the poor will need to be raised. Writing from the perspective of Third World countries, she succinctly concludes that the Christian non-poor of these times are called by the Gospel to release their grip on the things the poor need to survive. Relinquishment will be the predominant virtue of the Western Church in solidarity with the world's poor.[9]

---

[9] Marie Augusta Neal, *The Just Demands of the Poor* (New York: Paulist Press, 1986), p. 96.

A most compelling forecast of the identifying features of the coming Church appears in the work of Holland and Henriot. The analysis reported in the preface to their work, *Social Analysis: Linking Faith and Justice*, cuts deeper than Neal's to look at the crisis facing civilization as a whole. They summarize the direction of this civilization as one moving towards destruction on all levels and towards effacing the image of God from all human concerns.[10]

The polarized responses in the Church to this crisis are typified by these writers in terms that are reminiscent of the dichotomy in missiology already mentioned. Here, though, the poles are the transformation of society on the one hand and the appeal to religious transcendence on the other. Broadly these parallel the vertical-horizontal tensions of the missiology debate. Holland and Henriot call for a combination of these two solutions, the transformation of civilization through justice and the return to the spiritual roots of creative energies. The resulting communitarian society will be based on solidarity with the poor and a view of the material as being spirit-filled, they say.[11]

A specific element of this call deserves to be stressed here: the challenge given to religious by these writers to bond with the laity so that the prophetic witness which has been reserved to religious life in the past may now be shared with the whole Church. It is a gift required of all Christians by the present crisis.[12]

In summary, these analyses of the interaction of religion and society indicate the need for the witness of a Church committed to justice, to solidarity with the poor and to a rediscovery of the presence of God's Spirit in the entire creation; in short, the transformation of this world.

---

[10] Joe Holland and Peter Henriot, *Social Analysis: Linking Faith and Justice* (Maryknoll: Orbis Books, 1983), p. xiii.

[11] Ibid., p. xv.

[12] Ibid., p. xxi.

Of Justice and Love

One final brief comment should be made on the distinctions often made between justice and love. As human attributes, they defy neat definition. Yet since justice is seen in this book as a major concern of the Church in the coming years, it is necessary to attempt a more detailed description at least.

Justice is most often understood as an ordering of relationships so that the inherent equality of persons, races, and cultures is obvious in the transactions made between those groups. Often these relationships will have a more public quality to them, as in the case of economic justice. Of all the issues which might exemplify this description, that of the supposed equality of the sexes most graphically depicts the sense of this justice. Women's experience of inequality has given rise to a movement for the redress of their basic rights.

Some commentaries on justice seek to set up a dichotomy between justice and love so that, particularly among Christians, love is seen as a higher virtue, a more complete gift of oneself. Such a view is rejected in this book as creating an unnecessary dualism and leading in itself to new forms of injustice. Rather, justice is better appreciated as the strength of love, the rational quality that ensures that love is more than mere sentimentality.

Karen Lebacqz has drawn together six theories of justice from philosophical and theological circles, most of which center on the economic areas of transaction. Of these six, the closest to what is envisaged in this study occurs in the essays on Reinhold Niebuhr and José Porfirio Miranda.[13] Both of these seek the fusion of justice and love rather than their differentiation. While Niebuhr juxtaposes love and justice, he comes down to a marriage of the two in the concept of equality. If love is the final law of life, religion will

---

[13] Karen Lebacqz, *Six Theories of Justice* (Minneapolis: Augsburg Publishing House, 1986).

stultify if it does not support justice as the political and economic approximation of this ideal.[14]

Miranda's union of love and justice is more strongly forged. He argues that biblical love and justice are one and the same thing. There can be no justice without love and vice versa. He states that the differentiation between justice and love is one of the most disastrous errors in Christianity. Students of history could well agree.[15]

When justice is used in the following work, it carries the sense of equality in love. It therefore signifies the thought expressed by the verses from Micah:

> This is what Yahweh asks of you:
> only this,
> to act justly,
> to love tenderly
> and to walk humbly with your God (Mi 6:8).

---

[14] Ibid., p. 87.
[15] Ibid., p. 108.

Chapter Two

A NEED IN OUR TIMES

The mission of the Church finds its expression in the various ministries of individuals and groups to the larger world. The demands of the times and the needs of the Church require that the followers of the charism of Edmund Rice refound a ministry that is in keeping with a reformulation of his original mission. This must be a ministry or ministries responsive to the signs of the times.

The Congregation of the Christian Brothers was founded in response to the educational needs of the street kids in Waterford, Ireland. Over time this ministry became an education of both poor and well-to-do. More recently, there has been very little education of the poor, as schools rose in status with the very poor they had educated. The Brothers' schools would now be typified as middle-class in many places.

Studies of the phenomenon of "street kids," undertaken prior to this present work, have demonstrated the ubiquitous nature of the problem in today's world.[1] Three centers, viz. Brisbane, Australia; New York, USA; and Lima, Peru, have produced similar data, though the specifics of the phenomenon vary according to the conditions of the country. This suggests that the problem of children on the streets is worldwide.

---

[1] These studies were completed as follows: Australia, 1986 (Summer); New York, 1987 (Spring); Peru, 1987 (Summer).

Whereas in the First World this phenomenon remains somewhat hidden and denied, at least until very recently, the Third World manifestations in such places as Brazil, Bolivia, Peru, the Philippines and parts of Africa are all too evident. Of the children who enter elementary school in these places, only 20% continue into high school. Of these a marginal percentage finish and go on to college, most of them never completing courses.

Some argument for this state of affairs is made on the basis that children have to work in order to help support the family. While this is true, what is not said is that work just does not exist for most of the children most of the time. Their parents themselves find it difficult enough to get employment and to keep it. The obvious consequence is that these children are to be seen in their hundreds at any time of the day or night, roaming the streets of the *barrios* or playing somewhere around the home. They scrounge what food they can and take advantage of occasional chances to make a few *centavos*. Life promises little else.

It may seem a long way from the rough shanties of the *barrios* in Peru to the apartments and housing projects of Harlem or the Bronx in New York City. The contention of this book is that they are nonetheless both very much a part of the same world and the outcome of similar forces or evils within the societies in which they live.

Studies reveal a number of similarities between the young on the streets of New York or anywhere else in the West and those of the poorer nations. Both find themselves under the influence of forces beyond their control. Similarities include the limited education of those on the streets, their poor prospects for long term employment, and the economic and/or psychological distress of their parents. The major differences between the First and Third World locations are the massive resources at hand to deal with the problem in the First World compared with the poverty of the Third, and the resulting possibilities of some employment for a First World child.

Christian love, a love based on justice, demands that the

followers of the charism of Edmund Rice take cognizance of the thousands, indeed millions, world-wide who are today in the predicament of being children of the streets.[2]

Section 1

THE EDUCATION OF STREET KIDS

History of the Project

A review of the work of the Christian Brothers since 1985 in Brisbane, Australia on behalf of poor young people caught in the cycle of homelessness, truancy and crime began to suggest the need for an educational outreach along the lines of Paulo Freire models. Questions were raised about the value of traditional educational forms because of the widespread truanting among young people. Because of the parallels between these children and those to whom Edmund Rice had felt called, it was expected that this could be a ministry to which the Christian Brothers and those attracted by the charism of Edmund Rice could bring their professional teaching skills.

However, it was also soon recognized that these street kids formed a distinct culture, a sub-culture, within the main cultural norms. Anyone wanting to minister to this group would have to meet them on their own terms and learn the customs that existed among them and the motivations which maintained them in their relationship to society. As our analysis proceeded, it became obvious that these kids had as many grievances against society as society had against them. Many of their stories were of long years

---

[2] Susanna Agnelli, "Street Children: A Growing Urban Tragedy." *Report for the Independent Commission on International Humanitarian Issues* (London: Weidenfeld and Nicolson, 1986), p. 33.

of mistreatment by the various agencies of society, beginning always in the home.

The education of these street kids began to appear as a question of redressing injustices long tolerated by an unthinking society and of reknitting the societal framework of their lives.

Hypothesis

The growing number of street kids throughout the world, exemplified by the numbers of youngsters on the streets of New York, are potentially the poor, unemployed, divorced, drug addicted, and criminal adults of tomorrow. Robert Coles asserts in his study of youth in many parts of the world that "the majority of today's children live in ways that American writers and readers would consider to be wretched indeed."[3] For most of these young people, this choice is not their own. Circumstances have conspired through their short lives to leave them as the refuse of a society that is incapable of better dealing with its own pathologies. Teachers, among other professionals, are in the habit of attributing the term failure to those who come from unstable family backgrounds, have left school prematurely or are truanting, are unemployed and often enough take part in criminal activities. Their futures are bleak indeed.

Yet there are many involved in the ministry to these young people who see their condition as unnecessary suffering. Intervention is possible, they believe, to reverse this process, but it must be based on a clear analysis of the causes coupled with action to combat the problem at its most fundamental source. In this regard and in light of what has already been said, are these young people solely the responsibility of their parents? Or are there multiple reasons for

---

[3] Robert Coles, *The Moral Life of Children* (Boston: The Atlantic Monthly Press, 1986), p. 13.

this tragedy which suggest a systemic and even ideological base to their so-called failure?

The hypothesis is that the various agencies and institutions of society through which these youngsters have passed have conspired, albeit unintentionally at times, to reduce the young people's capacity to live with dignity in that society. If the same message is communicated to them by a number of institutions, these young people have no option but to accept it. What is perceived here is an oppression of society's most vulnerable and defenseless members, if not for the benefit of some other portion of society or of society as a whole, then surely out of unconscionable neglect.

In simple terms, parents, foster parents, welfare agencies, schools, law enforcement officers, peers and certain exploiters (i.e., drug dealers, pimps, etc.) in the child's life who prey on their vulnerability have given the child the message that he or she belongs on the streets.

The tools of social ethics will be used to attempt to verify this situation and to describe a possible intervention and reversal of the phenomenon.

Motives

Experience has shown that street kids are both victims and victimizers. As such they are no less human than the rest of society but through certain economic and sociological circumstances are placed in a set of conditions which result in anger, frustration, the inability to cope with life adequately, depression, violence and criminal activities, and the overriding inability to form lasting stable relationships and to see life as meaningful. Such a profile makes learning in the formal sense of education very difficult indeed. Hence the high truancy rate among such children (in Australia, for example, from seven years of age).

Paul Willis has demonstrated that, in England, the counterculture of "high school drop-outs" takes its cultural cues from the working class and transfers these to street and school life.[4] It has been our experience that street kids see themselves as an extension of one class of society, often with a criminal involvement. In so doing, they mimic the survival mechanisms of this group. Often their parents or relatives have modelled this behavior for them.

The Christian Brothers in Australia have observed that the families from which these young people emerge are invariably marred by many of the same traits and inadequacies as are exhibited by the child. In fact, there is a sense of an unending cycle in which the pattern of living of this present generation will be repeated by the next and so on with predictable outcomes unless major intervention is made early enough in the life of any child or group of children. We are therefore speaking about the prolongation of a whole class in society, since the families of these street kids are usually the poor and marginal members of society at present. If they are not one-parent families, then the condition of the primary relationship is already such that the family may be termed unhealthy.

Some have even gone so far as to suggest that labor-intensive societies require a class of poor so that the system as a whole may succeed and prosper. David Whisnat,[5] for example, quotes the paradigm of Daniel Patrick Moynihan which may be seen as relevant to the present discussion:

Corporate monopolization of resources
leads to
an inequitable and underdeveloped economic and
political system
which leads to
political powerlessness,

---

[4] Paul Willis, *Learning to Labor: How Working Class Kids Get Working Class Jobs* (New York: Columbia University Press, 1977).

[5] Cf. Michael Harrington, *The New American Poverty* (New York: Holt, Rinehart and Winston, 1984), p. 205.

> economic and cultural exploitation
> and environmental destruction
> which leads to
> poor education and social services,
> minimal income,
> hopelessness,
> and outmigration
> which facilitates further
> corporate monopolization of major resources.

It is our contention that not merely in the future as adults but even as children in the here and now, the youth of our streets have become the "new poor," the emerging class of dependents who ensure that the above paradigm operates. Along with women, the poor and the elderly, these youngsters have become in a deeper sense the "little ones" and the marginalized of society.

As Third World countries have discovered that the system must change if the poor are to have a place of equality and dignity in it, so it is our belief that the children of the streets must find their voice to protest this sub-cultural wastage. A sociological view of their plight demands changes which could challenge the very mechanism that spawns this phenomenon and could move towards its eradication.

Some Presuppositions

This analysis was undertaken with the following presuppositions in mind:

That home and the rest of society are so interdependent that much of the ideological script of society has already been absorbed in the home before the child has further contact with the other agencies of society.

That while the young people of the streets exhibit many

strengths including some quite moral attributes, their behavior is indicative of a great deal of personal suffering and of loss of meaning.

That human beings are a composite whole so that there is an interrelation of all levels of the person, social, moral, psychological and religious as well as the communal dimensions of relationship and meaning, history and culture.

That of the many agencies reviewed here, education has a special responsibility in the formation of the young since it acts as an initial bridge between the home and society and can critique the effect of one against the other and against the abstract value system by which the society or community functions.

Review of the Literature

Robert Coles uses the clinical tools of psychology to survey the life of children in the predicament described here. In his volumes on *Children in Crisis* he gives the results of numerous interviews with youngsters that highlight for us the dimensions of the problem. He demonstrates that no one simple structure can automatically produce a coping and even fulfilled human being. Furthermore, the influences on a child are so many and varied that birth into the most wretched circumstances does not automatically mean degradation. In many subtle and varied ways, every individual is capable of something better. Yet this only serves to underline further that without the limits imposed by poverty and oppression, a much happier life is possible.

For example, with regard to Black children in the southern states, he says that they have shown remarkable resilience and assertiveness in the right political climate. He argues that their tragedies do not start early in life at home but only commence when society begins to use color as a cause for restriction leading to the child's loss of individual worth and self-esteem.[6] (It should also be pointed out that children can encounter tragic situations in dysfunctional families.)

There is a strong sense in this statement of the systemic relationships between poverty, racism and the plight of uneducated children on the streets. It has been remarked in Australia that there is a higher percentage of Aboriginal children on the streets among the poor population than in the population at large. Coles identifies the tension for African Americans in achieving in a society which already has them culturally branded.

Harrington, Willis and others have researched the conditions that lead to the phenomenon of the urban poor and, in the case of Willis, of the ways in which one societal organization, that of education or the lack of it, perpetuates the injustices of the system that gives rise to the class of the urban poor from which street kids emerge. A most important contribution here is an understanding of the ideological underpinnings of such education or its denial.

Willis holds that the educational exchange parallels the basic exchange of capitalism where labor is bought and sold. He says that labor power is the only variable in the capitalist system and that it is the individual laborer's ignorance of the special nature of his commodity that makes him vulnerable. Education can change all that. Lack of education thus limits the worker's access to power over his or her own future. In later years, as an adult without education, this person will be a worthless commodity in the labor market.[7] Children are the first to be victimized by a lack of education. If Willis is correct, then it is high time that those involved in education took a critical look at the processes and outcomes of a lack of education in capitalist societies.

Illich and Freire offer not only a point of comparison with traditional forms of education as outlined by Willis but also the

---

[6] Robert Coles, *Children in Crisis: A Study of Courage and Fear* (Boston: The Atlantic Monthly Press, 1967), p. 367.

[7] Paul Willis, *Learning to Labor*, 1977, p. 130.

practical implementation of a form of "popular education" which of its essence can critique the values of the society and its ideological presuppositions. I would propose that their insights should be used to formulate a type of educational intervention in the cycle of poor neighborhoods in the First World just as it has been in the Third.

At the heart of "popular education" is dialogue, dialogue which is intended to allow the persons in the process to remain subjects of their own transformation. The ideals of this procedure as expressed by Freire make good reading for the underprivileged youngsters of our cities. The teacher is no longer merely the "one who teaches," but is himself or herself taught in dialogue with the students, who in turn while being taught also teach. There is joint responsibility for a process in which all grow. Arguments from authority are no longer valid since authority must now be on the side of freedom.[8]

Section 2
METHODS OF RESEARCH

In 1987, a series of interviews was conducted by the author in collaboration with Brother Peter Hancock who at the time was working on his doctoral thesis at Columbia University in New York. Peter had established a procedure for interviewing street kids using ethnographic methods of research from the discipline of cultural anthropology. The data elicited by Peter in these interviews has been used here to hypothesize a model of the interactions between these young people and the larger society. From the data, it was possible to prepare a social analysis which could then be tested by the author using a participatory interview technique with the young people of Covenant House, New York.

---

[8] Paulo Freire, *Pedagogy of the Oppressed* (New York: Herder and Herder, 1968), p. 67.

The entire process combined methods from anthropology and sociology in the development of an educational response to street kids. The next three sections, following Peter's description of his work, report this process. Section 3 is a distilling of the social implications of Peter's material. Section 4 proposes a model to explain this analysis and Section 5 tests the analysis with the young people of Covenant House.

Peter's own description situates his interviews in their geographic and demographic context:

"The setting for the primary participant observation is the very solid, very stationary four-storey, two wing, main bus terminal for Manhattan.

"Through this building pass thousands of buses, millions of people each day. Set between 8th and 9th Avenues, and 40th and 42nd Streets, it serves a vital function in the transport network for New York City.

"At the fringes of the business community has gathered another community: the drug-dealers, the muggers, the prostitutes, the hustlers, peddlers and the beggars whose livelihood too is related to the presence of the tourists."[9]

It is easily seen that any process that required entering into this fringe community as an observer would be beset with difficulties. Peter continues his narrative:

"When I was loitering, trying to observe the people and their interactions, from the safety of the public space of the corridors, I often found myself in conversation with another loiterer. I decided early that I would explain myself and my task, if I thought there was any chance that the person would respond simply to a greeting, with a 'Hi!', realizing that there was an expectation I would have to dispel, that I was a customer."[10]

---

[9] P. Hancock, *Education in the Streets: An Ethnographic Study of Homeless Youth in New York City* (Ann Arbor, MI: University Microfilms International, 1988), p. 31.

[10] Ibid., p. 36.

I am grateful to Peter for the risks he took and the significant material that emerged in his taped interviews of the young people inhabiting this rather shadowy world. As he says, he did not offer case studies as such nor attempt to typify the "street kid" but allowed individual youngsters to speak for themselves. We meet some of these in the next section as I begin to analyze the social dimensions of some excerpts from their statements.

Section 3

AN ANALYSIS OF THE INTERACTION OF STREET KIDS WITH SOCIETY'S INSTITUTIONS

The following interviews with street kids in New York were conducted over a period of months during 1987. Comments from the transcriptions of taped interviews have been collated according to the various agencies of society that have mediated the world to these young people. Interviewees were encouraged to talk about what had led them to the streets, how they survived there, and what they hoped for the future.

Home

There is a pervasive sense here in the interviews of the abuse of young people in family life, though the guilt seems to be experienced as much by the youth as one would hope it is by the adult. Drugs and alcohol are invariably key factors in the dysfunctioning of these families and provide the temporary solution to all problems for the adolescent as well. The feeling of having "been used" by the family is all too prevalent.

Will: "I got into drugs... I lost my family." "I stole from my mother... that's the worst thing I ever regretted." "I felt

A Need in Our Times

bad... it was her money to eat... She noticed then, 'If he did it to me, how many people is he going to do it to?' We talked."

Frank: "They was all alcohol related... it was real bad. I used to get beaten to death when I was little... I ran away."

Joe: "She started using drugs. She started putting me out of the house, telling me, 'Go out and make money for the rent, for the food I'm eating.'" "She wants me to make money to pay for her." "She wanted me to go out on the street and hustle. She doesn't give a f... about me." "I want to teach her a lesson." ("Father?") "I haven't got one."

School

This institution is often seen as a sign of hope by street kids. They can recount many examples of bad experiences and of feelings of worthlessness but there is the realization that overall teachers are there to help them. There is good reason to use this as an agency for change in their lives.

Will: "I want to get back to school."

Joe: "So eventually I want to go to Covenant House and go back to school... 'cause I know if I don't do something good for myself, nobody's going to do it for me."

Peers

Street kids require love. Their lives are filled with failed relationships. The inadequacies of the home transfer to the streets.

Will: "They're into crack, that's why they're all f....d up. They can't do anything."

Frank: "I didn't care about nobody but myself..." "Now I wish I had a friend, and there was one I couldn't hold onto... I ripped him off."

Joe: "The people that I loved before turned my love to hate." "There could be guys out there just looking at her that already have got to her. I'll take her as a friend, but that is about it."

Welfare Agencies

As with all street people, there is a reliance on the social welfare system for the basic necessities of life: food, shelter, clothing, rehabilitation. This is simply one further demeaning episode in the life of a youngster. To have to be dependent at this time in life when the purpose of being on the street was to gain independence must be a galling and humiliating experience.

Frank: "I'm possibly going to a rehab center... it'll be my first time... I really hope I get something out of it this time... probably it'll be better this time... I get sick and tired of being sick and tired." "The Salvation Army is very religious... they got all these programs... I hope it works this time."

Joe: "The foster mother saw that and started whipping him with a wire... she was f...n' him up." "I've been in eight foster homes."

Entrepreneurs

Contrasting with the failure to get and maintain jobs is the money that can be earned by these youngsters in the variety of ways they are forced (or choose) to sell themselves. The exorbitant

A Need in Our Times

rewards for such behavior that are quoted here need not be totally untrue. But one must realize that the condition of these youngsters most of the time belies the idea that they could be receiving such recompense regularly. Often though they are able to buy the occasional set of clothes or have a decent meal. The children around Times Square are usually dirty and look undernourished.

Will: "You come down here to hustle but people want to take you as suckers... you know... you tell 'em $15-$20 but they only want to give you $5 or give you crack... I tell 'em no, so they get upset." "You don't get treated right down here. This place is bad in the day time, it's bad in the night time... before someone would take you, they'd pick you up and take you home... Now since the crack you don't trust nobody." "I take a shower... do what we gotta do... in the morning I get paid."

Joe: "A week, five thousand dollars. I go to hotels. $60 to go there a night." "I go to 53rd and 3rd. There's millionaires, directors, executives." "They want something for fifteen minutes."

Some Reactions

Will: "You think about it. You think about suicide." "You always need people... my mother's the only person I've really got... I'd never tell her about hustling."

Frank: "I felt bad about it..." "I been doing a lot of thinking... drugs, friendships... didn't trust nobody... you start to learn more about yourself."

Joe: "I just want to be independent and responsible." "I see that I'm out here... I have nobody. I don't think that nobody should be out here, nobody at all..." "F....d up. You've got to watch your back all the time... You can't trust nobody at all." "Where the hell am I going?"

Section 4

DIAGNOSIS

It has been suggested that there is an emerging "*pedism*" (from the Greek, *paiz*: a child, either son or daughter), just as there is racism, sexism or ageism. It amounts to *the exploitation of children* by elements of society so that the economic system may be better served. How it functions may be described best in the following terms:

When a child has established in the home that he or she is unloved or is loved only as a utility, there is an interaction with society that is developed and is carried forward into every other organ of that society. The child presumes that he or she is to be a possession rather than a person, a commodity rather than a being, an object rather than a subject, in every encounter with the social world. As psychologists are quick to point out, a person remains unlovable until told otherwise. If real love is not experienced, the negotiations commenced in the home may eventually issue in hustling, drug addiction, stealing and the many other ways in which street kids negotiate as products or consumers.

The sociological explanation could be diagrammed as shown.

The Diagram

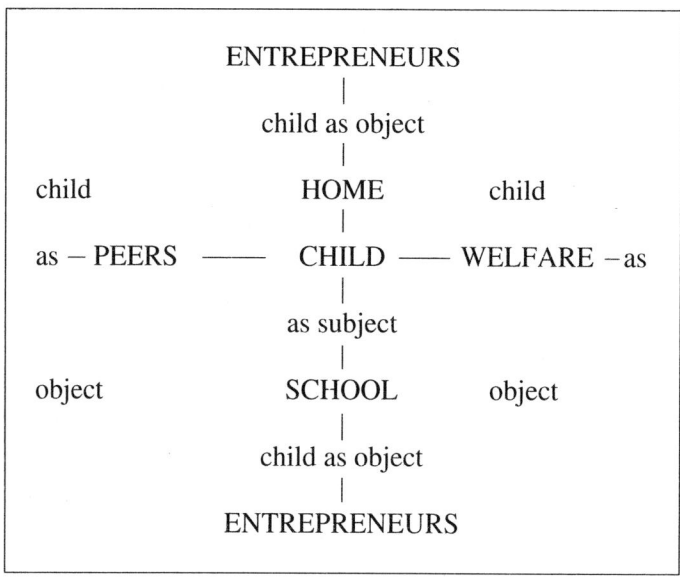

The child has taken his or her original self-understanding (I am merely a commodity, expendable, commercially viable but personally worthless) from the home to the only place where such a concept makes sense, to the streets. Rather than considering him/herself as a subject (in Freire's terms), he or she has now become an object and is vulnerable to treatment as such by the other agencies of society. These compound the misapprehension of self as worthless. There is a gradual movement to the streets since this is where the commodity of self is most useful and there are many people waiting to take advantage of this naivety.

Why is there such a conspiratorial silence on this issue? It would be appropriate if at least one of society's institutions could begin to reverse this trend.

Section 5
A MODEL FOR ACTION

The model for action described and tested in this section emerged directly from the analysis of the situation of street kids described in the Diagnosis. Given the claim for a structural basis for their plight, it was proposed that education, as one of the agencies of society charged with some moral purpose, could assist in the renewal of those structures and provide intervention in the cycle of oppression affecting these youngsters. No teacher would be glib enough to suggest that education alone would suffice. Too many factors exist which have bearing on the situation. However, education remains a key agent because of its link to the home and to other agencies of society and its role in transmitting cultural norms.

The model tested in this phase confirmed the analysis offered in the Diagnosis and suggested that other more specialized interventions such as welfare and crisis work were wholly inadequate to address the problem in the long term. It revealed that a greater effort at societal renewal and at prevention is necessary and that education is seen by the young people themselves as a key agent in their rehabilitation.

The investigation was conducted by using the process of participatory research to allow the subjects of the investigation themselves to shape the solution to their problems. As will be demonstrated, there is much in this approach, already well used in Third World countries, which is conducive to liberation and which fits well into the educational theories of Freire and Illich and others.

An Ethical Analysis

Moral values are foundational to this study and are an underlying assumption in the use of education as the intervening agency, as claimed above. Section 3 has shown that the young caught without an education in the structure of a highly sophisticated technological and labor-intensive society suffer the consequences of a structural oppression that at its worst preys on their vulnerability and encourages what can only be termed "pedism," the exploitation of children. Their value as human beings is reduced to the equivalent of a consumer item. They are merely products to be bought and sold as commodities. The Gospel itself condemns such a way of looking at these "little ones."

> "Are you not worth much more...?" (Mt 6:27).

and again,

> "I tell you solemnly, unless you change and become like little children..." (Mt 18:3-4).

> "See that you never despise any of these little ones..." (Mt 18:10).

It is to be expected then that Christian social ethics would advocate a model of action designed to challenge such oppression; to reveal, for what it is, the greed of those who through drugs, sex, exploitative wages, capitalize on the vulnerability of these young people; and to shape a means of empowering these youth.

The social justice statements of the Church provide further confirmation, if it is needed, of the Christian response to the street youth phenomenon — and once again, this happens within the ambit of a truly liberating education.

> Part of the human family lives immersed in a mentality which exalts possessions. The school and the communications media, which are often obstructed by the established order, allow the formation only of the person desired by that order, that is to say, the man or woman in its image, not a new person but a copy of the man or woman as he or she is.

But education demands a renewal of heart, a renewal based on the recognition of sin in its individual and social manifestations. It will also inculcate a truly and entirely human way of life in justice, love and simplicity. It will likewise awaken a critical sense, which will lead us to reflect on the society in which we live and on its values... In the developing countries, the principal aim of this education for justice consists in an attempt to awaken consciences to a knowledge of the concrete situation and in a call to secure a total improvement; by these means the transformation of the world has already begun. The content of this education necessarily involves respect for the person and for his or her dignity.[11]

Not only developing countries but the oppressed and alienated minorities of developed countries are in need of this transformation.

The Model in Action

Covenant House, Times Square, New York was chosen as the venue for the investigation because a relatively stable environment was needed to facilitate conversation with these street kids and to maximize the involvement of as many youngsters as possible.

The interviewer prepared for this research by discussing with community workers from Covenant House the rationale behind their intervention and the means by which it was accomplished. This happened over a number of meetings so that the final research method to be used would best suit the environment and yet be sufficiently independent to achieve complete freedom of speech with the young people. They were to perceive the interviewer as

---

[11] Gremillion (ed.), *Justice in the World*, Synod of Bishops Rome 1971 in *The Gospel of Peace and Justice* (Maryknoll: Orbis Books, 1976).

another of the adults who were available to them as helper in their time at Covenant House. This option was preferred over that of merely entering as a researcher because it was hoped that the youngsters themselves could benefit more directly this way and that the realism engendered would give greater validity to the test.

Time was spent in becoming familiar with the Times Square "street scene" prior to the interviews, noting the numbers of young people on the street, their condition, their refuges and their cognizance of the availability of help. It was noted that even in the Times Square area itself, young people on the street did not know the address of Covenant House when asked. Most of its residents were either referrals or were taken in by the nighttime outreach service. The conclusion could be reached that to go to Covenant House meant one had "hit bottom."

The Participatory Interviews

Of the many conversations that were conducted in the course of this research only two are reported here as being the best samples of the process that is envisaged in this model of action. One of these occurred on the floor of the young (between 14 and 16 years old) male residents, the other was an interview with various staff, helpers, and young people (themselves ex-street kids) who were on night duty at the shelter during this same visit. In the future use of this process, these two groups would be combined so that staff and youngsters dialogue about their common problems. The two groups in this experiment were as yet unready for this and, since change would be a likely outcome, a visitor was not in the position to ask this of them.

The object of the dialogue with the residents, the street kids themselves, was to stimulate as nearly as possible the dialogue that could be established with a group of truanting young people about the role of education in their lives, with the belief that they could begin to reshape that model if they so desired. Such a revised model would incorporate their best insights about society and the role of education which surfaced in the course of the dialogue.

Since this dialogue was rather laborious and at times circuitous, only the major turning points in the discussion are recorded here with interlocking commentary and report by the interviewer.

After the report on the first dialogue, conclusions will be drawn before referring to the second, the discussion with the staff.

A Dialogue with a Group of New York Street Kids

What commenced here with two individuals concluded with the involvement of the whole floor of some thirty youngsters as will be noted. Only relevant parts of the dialogue are included.

The approach of the interviewer brought a ready response from the young men sitting on the floor in silence. After introductions, Andrew began unprompted.

Andrew: These people here are wild. They might look alright now, but I can tell you on the streets they're wild.
Int.: And what about yourself, Andrew?
Andrew: *My family just used me. Everybody's been using me.*

The significance of this beginning caused the interview to digress onto the experiences which had evoked this sense of worthlessness, of being perceived as a mere commodity to be used. Andrew said quite simply that he had meant little to his mother. She had done everything but take money from him; he had not known his father though he had a number of "step-fathers." He had been sent to live with his brother but when he was again seen as an inconvenience, he left and came to New York. Andrew later revealed that he was under psychiatric care because of his aggressive tendencies and admitted that this had played a part in his running away.

The interviewer introduced the idea of school, and Andrew smiled for the first time.

Andrew: I was good at art in school. *The teacher displayed my work* on the walls. I still have it....

Others, who had been sitting nearby and had allowed the conversation to progress without showing any particular inclination to be involved, began to show interest. Anthony had been doodling all the while on a portrait of some face which later revealed itself as that of a transvestite. I sought to involve him and he showed interest immediately. So I asked him to let me take his art with me as a sample of what young people on the streets here can do. He was suitably touched by the implied compliment. After testing that I really wanted it, he promised it to me at the end of the night when it was completed.

Not to be outdone, Andrew attracted attention with another reference to school.

Andrew: I want to go back to school.
Int.: Where did you go to school?
Andrew: All over, but mainly upstate. It was better than being on the streets.
Anthony: No. I don't think it is.
Andrew: You're crazy, man. This is boring.
Anthony: You can have fun here.
Andrew: *School's easy for you.* (Anthony nodded in agreement.)

We proceeded to discuss the influence of "crack" on the lives of these young men. They asserted that it was part of the fun on the streets and yet the very threat that now made school so attractive to Andrew. Both presumed that I appreciated that they would have been involved with it. Only one of them showed signs of wanting to relinquish it. I brought the conversation back to the topic of school.

Int.: Did you do art in school?
Anthony: Yeah. I liked art. (An argument developed immediately between these two on the differences between the art forms they preferred.)
Anthony: *Art should be creative. Not like that...* (pointing to the pages I'd noticed Andrew periodically perusing).
Andrew: *No! You learn from copying these.* I do it all the time. (Anthony seems to doubt this.)

I now realized that what Andrew held were magazine photos of prints from such masters as Raphael and Michelangelo, not the kind of material one would expect to find in the hands of a street kid. Their argument over the relative values of the different forms of learning art continued for some time. Eventually they were interrupted.

Michael, who had been standing nearby the whole time, now entered the conversation. He thrust his own sketch on the table in front of me. I commented favorably on it, then asked,

Int.: Did you do art at school?
Michael: Yeah, but I didn't like it. (Then, with some anger...) *You can only do construction at school.* I'd prefer to paint things like Picasso.

Michael's whole bearing was of somebody who meant what he said. His sketch had a commensurate finesse that Anthony's lacked, I thought. His anger at the stifling effects of his education had a poignancy, especially after hearing the affirming nature of Andrew's experience. I did not doubt Michael's desire to paint exactly as he said and perhaps, given the right encouragement, his ability one day to accomplish it. I reflected on where he might have developed these interests. At home or in discussion with those he "served" on the streets? Whichever it was, he had learned much about art already, *outside the main stream of education.*

The conversation was interrupted by the evening meeting. I

reminded Anthony that when we returned he'd promised to give me his drawing on which he had continued to work throughout this time. Michael immediately volunteered his and I accepted. It was discomforting to go from this discussion to the first item of the meeting: "It is an offense to carry a weapon here, so you are asked to turn in all weapons before you go to bed."

When we returned the whole floor was again gathered in the recreation room. I asked Anthony for his art. He seemed close to tears and just held out empty hands. His sketch was obviously missing. The rest of the group began to offer suggestions as to where he might have put it and some as to where he should.... It was not long before another fight was in progress, and only my withdrawal reduced the tension. I noticed Anthony return to his own group, still accusing others of taking it.

I looked in the paper bin nearby and found the two sample sketches I had requested. Anthony and Michael both looked very pleased when they saw I'd recovered them, and this immediately seemed to reestablish their credibility with the group. I withdrew.

Some Conclusions

This simple dialogue demonstrates many of the themes already evoked in the first half of this study. Much of the material here is familiar to any classroom teacher. However, because of the questioning of school procedures that is implied, the conversation would rarely be allowed to develop to this extent, much less to proceed beyond it. There is an obvious threat to good order, to the status quo, if one were to pursue the line of thought introduced by Michael.

Was there a good reason for his not being allowed to study Picasso? Did anyone ever ask his interests? What would happen if the school tried to follow the interests of every child? Would there eventually be fewer "hyperactive" children, fewer truants, more affirmed students like Andrew?

There may be something to be said for the system operating in East Harlem district schools where children *choose* their own educational establishment based on the courses offered: the school of science, or music, or math, or art. Attendance and grades have improved noticeably since the system was introduced.

But there are more fundamental questions raised by this dialogue. These young people were doing in their spare time at Covenant House what a number of art teachers had presumably spent much time encouraging at school, i.e., they were developing a love of art. Through their activity they were able to resist the desire to spend the night in the fruitless activities of the street and, in the presence of an adult, to gain the individual and group acceptance so crucial to their further personal development. Of their own accord they had learned something of the great masters of the art world and had done so in a more immediate way than would many in the history of art courses that are traditionally a part of school curricula.

The significance of this dialogue in reference to the conclusions of the section, Diagnosis, given earlier in this book may be obvious. The youngsters themselves reiterated the findings of that phase. Andrew spoke in precisely those terms — he saw himself as a consumer item, a commodity, an object. Against this can be contrasted the needs of the whole group, in the Model-for-Action section of this study, for affirmation and their ready acceptance of it when offered, even if given obliquely as in the case of asking for the sketches. The derision given the two artists whose work had been mislaid was commonplace for such emotionally deprived youngsters. They were being reminded that they were *only* street kids.

Michael's questioning of the system now takes on further significance. What happened in the brief course of one evening's dialogue could become the paradigm for a new way of learning for these young people. If an institution were free to question its own operations and those of the other agencies in society — the home, the legal, the welfare, the medical system, the Church and even government itself — a very different state of affairs may ensue for these young people. If such critical dialogue could be established between the child and each agency a new social dynamic would emerge, one in which the youngster could reclaim some of the power over his own life so blatantly taken from him or her in the initial stages of ego definition and so crudely retained by the pimps, johns and drug dealers.

This dialogue demonstrates that, if asked what needs to be changed for them to live satisfying lives, street kids could eventually reshape their own environment, at least in theory. Would the adult world be willing to grant them this empowerment? My own belief is that this can happen if some adults begin to stand with the youngsters in just such honest and liberating relationship.

Some Practical Dimensions of This Model

To commence a participatory research project with a group of truants, given the above experience, would require:

The longterm commitment of teachers entering the dialogue.

Small numbers of truants per teacher so that group and individual concerns could be followed through.

A structure, institution or environment that was extremely flexible and open to contact with the wider community.

A willingness to involve other staff, parents and significant adults from the community in the dialogue.

A fearless commitment by all in the program to search for truth together and to seek the empowerment of the group, despite the threat to the established order that would ensue.

The Interview with Covenant House Staff

To give further flesh to the possible outcomes of such a procedure, the perceived benefits were tested with some of the staff at Covenant House following the interviews with the youngsters. Present were a variety of adults from lay volunteers to ex-street kids, employed community workers and a religious Sister. Michael's attitude to the educational system was cited to them as evidence of the young people's felt disenchantment with the agencies through which they had passed before ending in their present predicament. The question resolved itself to what could be done to reshape education.

Some of the staff revealed their own dissatisfaction with the crisis intervention provided by their own agency. They referred to the youngsters as *"corporate bunnies."* Even Covenant House, it was seen, bought into the dominant ideology of the society, that success depended on having money and that persons would be seen as functional by that society only in terms of wealth or the ability to procure it. The goal set young people at Covenant House was to get out by getting employment. This was very much crisis treatment rather than preventative work, some workers said.

Among the comments were:

"The system is counter-productive. Our society prefers to build jails rather than schools."

"These kids need to be stopped for a while; to be at peace for a minute. It can't happen on the streets here. They need to be taken away from here. The peer pressure here is phenomenal."

"Social workers are giving up. No one wants to take this on." (Referring to the Times Square situation.)

"For these kids, success is synonymous with clothes; even the worst kids here have good clothes. Their role models are the pimps!"

A Need in Our Times

Section 6

A NEW EDUCATIONAL MODEL

What has emerged from this series of interviews and is evident to some degree in the foregoing material is the structural injustice that is perpetrated in the name of education. Admittedly, it is only one of the institutions that is used by society to achieve its aims. But it is one that by its very nature should bring a critical judgment to the process of transmission of knowledge and values. One may ask to what extent true education can be permitted to foster the kind of oppression that is evident in the lives of the young people interviewed in the above situation.

Some elements of schooling which would appear to be extensions of the societal creed and yet inimical to the youngsters interviewed in this work are as follows:

> The excessive emphasis on a uniform system of advancement and on homogeneous groupings according to age.

> The cult of the individual which permeates society and yet is allowed to dominate the educational process to such an extent that students find little affirmation in school aside from the occasional comments of teachers.

> The demand for academic excellence at the expense of other more human qualities.

> The correlation between economic realities and the students' "success" or "failure."

> The oftentimes inflexible, introverted and non-reflective nature of the educational process.

A Liberating Education

The suggestion has been made and supported by the evidence of the dialogue with people from the streets of New York that a structural intervention is necessary to reverse the trend to produce youngsters who can have no other place in society than that of the oppressed and alienated street youth. It has been suggested that this oppression approaches "pedism." A model for action has been developed around the use of participatory research which would begin a review of the educational model and then of its interaction with other agencies of society. Fundamental to this renewal would be the very dialogue commenced by the research itself.

In *Pedagogy of the Oppressed*, Paulo Freire uses a similar approach to awaken the consciousness of students and teachers to the kind of oppression they are experiencing in Third World countries. Much of what he says could as well apply to the model that is emerging here. In a recent update of his thesis, *A Pedagogy for Liberation: Dialogues on Transforming Education*, Freire shares with Ira Shor the insights that each has had about such an education since the first publication. A quotation from them is a fitting conclusion.

> The criticism that liberating education has to offer emphatically is not the criticism which ends at the subsystem of education. On the contrary, the criticism in the liberatory class goes beyond the subsystem of education and becomes a criticism of society.[12]

---

[12] P. Freire and I. Shor, *A Pedagogy for Liberation: Dialogues on Transforming Education* (South Hadley, MA: Bergin and Garvey Publishers, Inc., 1987), p. 35.

EXTENSIONS

Two studies were conducted to extend the thesis proposed here. The first consisted in a visit to South America to compare this material with the situation of street children in Lima, Peru; the second was a brief study of the links between truanting or unemployed children on the street and the incidence of women as heads of households among the poor in Westchester County, New York.

Peru

In interviews with the children of Miraflores in Lima, it was established that these youngsters were not necessarily neighborhood children but had themselves arrived in this wealthier part of town from the *barrios*, looking for work. They found it in this section with any position from shoe-shining to prostitution. Children were proud of their adaptability in being able to accommodate themselves to a number of tasks.

The evidence here suggests that the youth of Lima are as apt to be treated as commodities as are the youth of New York at the center of the free world. While many New York youngsters leave home primarily because of family breakdown which may in turn be associated with poverty, the children of Lima do so more frequently because of the direct results of poverty, especially hunger. Parents in Lima often send their children to work at an early age.

An investigation was made of the unions organized for these young workers by Alejandro Cussianovich, a priest-worker. Most surprising was the finding that apart from the thousands of youngsters gaining the strength of their union for protection from those who would exploit them, Cussianovich has organized schools with lay (non-teacher) volunteers. He apparently believes that long term relief from their plight is really in their own hands, especially since his model of education is based on Freire.

Evidence suggests the Third World phenomenon of street

youth has a basis in the same causes as occur in the First World, though exacerbated immensely by the sheer poverty of the regions. Pedism exists as much in Lima as in New York.

Westchester County

Results of an analysis of women and children in the bands of poverty in New York showed a high incidence of both women who were heads of households and truanting children. Further, they confirmed that these problems resulted from a combination of the effects of racism, sexism and pedism on the community of the poor. Connections were made through statistics and through interviews of residents of the town of Ossining.

Shortly after the completion of this study a national demographic report was released which confirmed the nature of these results.[13] It showed that the two major identifying characteristics of the poor in America are, first, women as heads of house (some 60% of poor women) and second, children unemployed or truanting and therefore on the streets (some 40% of the children). It is believed these figures have significance for a ministry to street children, since it has been shown that there is an interlocking of the various agencies of society in the oppression of youth. If pedism and sexism are both at work in this systemic injustice, the need for a forthright stand in solidarity with the poor, especially in urban areas, becomes an educational imperative.

---

[13] Reported in *The New York Times*, Dec. 20, 1987, p. 26.

Concluding Remarks

It has been shown that there is a critical need for an intervention in the lives of New York street kids and that this may be indicative of the needs of such youngsters world wide.

The problem has been seen to have an ethical and social base and therefore, if education is to be used as the intervening tool, it must be shaped by the dimensions of the problems that have come to light here. In particular, a community education that offers the young the power to change their social situation is essential.

The problem has been seen to extend to the Third World and to encompass the phenomenon of single parent families as well.

Chapter Three

EDMUND RICE — LIBERATOR

*He may justly be called the Liberator
— such title he deserved.*[1]

Preamble

There is no attempt here to reduce Edmund's life and ministry to one aspect only. Rather, there is an attempt to recover something in his life, as it has come to us through biographers, historians and eulogizers, that may be significant for our times and that may broaden the picture of Edmund traditionally communicated within the Christian Brothers. If biographers have not attached the same importance to Edmund's mission as liberator, one possible reason is that the Church itself was not capable of appreciating this dimension of the Gospel to the same extent in the past.

Nor is there an attempt here to write a definitive and exhaustive treatment of the subject. That may not be possible until the Brothers and their co-workers themselves have lived for some time with a renewed image of Edmund and have tried to incorporate this

---

[1] From the letter of James J. Healy in M.C. Normoyle's *Memoirs of Edmund Rice*, for private circulation, 1979, p. 127.

into their own life and work. The emphasis in this chapter is on rediscovering elements that have been present in the tradition but have been overlooked or deemphasized. Coupled with the following scriptural reflection, this re-reading may prompt a renewed understanding of the Edmund Rice foundation.

The Ireland of Edmund's Day

In what sense was Edmund a liberator? To understand Edmund in this vein, it is necessary to situate him in the context of Ireland in the 18th and 19th centuries. The present conflicts in Northern Ireland are testimony to the bitterness and resentment aroused in the whole of Ireland over the entire period of British domination. From the time of Cromwell, this antipathy took a predominantly religious tone. As is so often the case in the subjugation of a people, religion was used as a *cause célèbre* with which to endorse increasingly harsh English controls. Yet Protestant and Catholic were divided on a much less lofty principle: that of wealth.

That economic factors as well as colonization were the prime cause of the English occupation of Ireland is well attested in history. Even in Cromwell's time, as W.C. Abbott wrote, plunder, the employment of the military and the desire to colonize were the major factors operating.[2] As England entered further into the Industrial Revolution, any land, even the most arid, could be a source of wealth through the growing of cotton, the raising of sheep or simply the siting of factories.

Successive sets of penal laws in 1695 and 1704-15 completed the annexation of Ireland by England, begun a century earlier. Parliamentary representation by the Irish, the vast majority of them Catholic, was to be denied them until 1829. The rape of what had

---

[2] James Carty, *Ireland 1607-1782* (Dublin: C.J. Fallon Ltd., 1958), p. 67.

been a wealthy country was begun in earnest. Even Irish Protestants who could afford to do so were forced to flee to America.[3]

But for Catholics it was worse. The penal laws had excluded them from public life. Catholic education was forbidden. Estates were subdivided and no new land could be purchased by a Catholic. In 1699, the export of woolen goods was forbidden to any country except England. Little wonder that a Lord Chief Justice could say, "The law does not presume any such person to exist as an Irish Catholic."[4]

Too poor to leave, the Catholics did begin to resist the new persecution. A committee was formed for relief against the laws and by 1762 their repeal was assured. But this had not occurred before the first of the devastating potato famines had stripped the country of the essential form of sustenance and some 400,000 had died.

It is therefore understandable that when Edmund was born in 1762, biographers relate, the poor were everywhere. In his local Callan, 1000 of the 2000 adults were unemployed. As in the rest of Ireland, begging had become a way of life for many. *The Querist* asked "whether there could be on the face of the earth any Christian or civilized people so beggarly, wretched and destitute as the common Irish."[5]

Born to Wealth

The Rices had land. Edmund's own family had a farm, including crops and cattle at Callan in County Kilkenny. Edmund's uncle Michael was particularly wealthy, being a merchant in Waterford. It was to this business that Edmund was attracted as he

---

[3] James Carty, *Ireland 1783-1850* (Dublin: C.J. Fallon Ltd., 1953), p. xvi.

[4] Desmond Rushe, *Edmund Rice: The Man and His Times* (Dublin: Gill and Macmillan, 1981), p. 6.

[5] Ibid., p. 7.

grew and completed the education that was denied so many of his countrymen and women. The fact that the Rices could afford to pay for the education he received already set him apart. This good fortune was then compounded when Michael accepted Edmund into the provisions trade.

Because of the nature of the business, Edmund quickly became an accepted member of social gatherings in Waterford. He married Mary Elliott, the daughter of another wealthy family when he was 23 years of age. Tragedy struck when Mary was killed, reportedly in a hunting accident early in 1789. The daughter the couple was expecting was saved but not without signs of retardation. The promising life and career that Edmund had carefully nurtured was abruptly and rudely interrupted.

But for the time being, Edmund's business life did not change and he continued to amass an amount of money that would have been considered a fortune by most Catholics. However, his wife's death had caused changes. Biographers note that he began to increase his "practice of prayer, reading and works of charity."[6] It was just two years after Mary's death that Edmund procured a copy of the Douay Bible and later inscribed its first page with a series of texts "concerned principally with those sections that had special reference to his daily work."[7]

The ten years following the procurement of the Bible have been described by biographers as a time of conversion. Certainly by the end of the decade Edmund's life had changed direction in a radical manner, but this took place gradually. The contention of this book is that the texts written in Edmund's Bible so near to this time of decision-making give valuable insight into the motivation for the actions of the ensuing years. Because of their importance, they will be treated separately.

---

[6] M.C. Normoyle, *A Tree Is Planted: The Life and Times of Edmund Rice*, private circulation, 1976, p. 28.
[7] Ibid., p. 30. The texts bear the entry "1823" next to them.

Usury in Ireland

Biographers indicate that the subject of Edmund's biblical reflection during this period, usury, was very much a part of the merchant's way of life in Ireland. The provisions trade was flourishing and Catholic merchants held a considerable amount of the supply of available money. They were in a position to exercise great local influence as the chief moneylenders.[8]

The moneys were loaned to people already in the grip of a depressed economy with very little hope of returning it. The poor were in the traditionally powerless position, vulnerable to unscrupulous creditors. As one of the class of merchants profiting from this situation, Edmund found it necessary to take cognizance of their actions.[9]

Edmund's biographers seem to imply that he had little personal reason for conversion. However, the realities of usury suggest that the practice was quite pervasive within his own class. The scriptural texts suggest his great concern about the effects of usury in his society. One is left to wonder about the extent of Edmund's participation in the practice.

Relinquishment

As well as Scripture, both prayer and works of charity began to shape a new life for Edmund. These three practices did not occur in isolation. The relaxation of laws against religion that occurred with the repeal of the penal laws encouraged the flourishing of Catholic societies. Edmund and his wealthy peers were among the

---

[8] A.L. O'Toole, *A Spiritual Profile of Edmund Ignatius Rice*, Vol. I: *More Than Silver or Gold* (Bristol: The Burleigh Press, 1984), p. 44.

[9] Ibid., p. 44.

first to take advantage of this. They, of course, had the time and education to do so.

> It was not too difficult to be a good young man in such a supportive environment where religion formed the accepted framework of the comfortable lifestyle of the well-to-do Catholic merchant class.[10]

The "works of charity" carried out by Edmund in this period need to be appreciated, though, for their growing commitment and breadth of public witness. Most of these works involved the dispensing of funds from Edmund's own purse. There was the case of "Black Johnny," a young man whose release he negotiated with the ship's captain and then was sent to the Sisters for an education. He completed the act by buying him a small house.

Edmund visited the jails and found them cold, wretched places. Many were in jail as debtors because of rising rents and the failure of the banks. Others were sentenced for political crimes. In 1799 he witnessed the death of a clerical student, Francis Hearn, on suspicion of being connected with the United Irishmen. Edmund himself saved the husband of his step-sister from execution for angering the militia.

"In 1798 the yeomen surrounded his home at midnight and, not having found him, set fire to the house and traced him to Waterford. Edmund hid him in his own home — a capital offense — until a suitable opportunity arrived to smuggle him in a barrel aboard a vessel bound for Newfoundland."[11] One of Edmund's many account books records the funds spent on donations to the jail through collections and directly in his visits there.

Much could also be said on Edmund's long and frequent periods of solitude at this time, though it is not directly appropriate

---

[10] Ibid., p. 29.
[11] Ibid., p. 82.

to the subject in hand. It is enough to recall that one of the possible choices that faced him towards the end of the 1790's was to retire to Rome and commit himself to the contemplative vocation. While biographers speak of the influence of his step-sister in the final decision to stay and care for the poor boys of Waterford, it is important to remember that this was already a work he had begun to undertake as part of his charities.

The youth on the streets of Waterford had long attracted his attention. They are described as "wild and uncared-for boys who daily gathered around the timber stacks on the Quay."[12] There were some 1000 of them in the city and most congregated near the docks, the merchant business area. Edmund visited the slums to reach out to them and was concerned by their lack of education in general and their lack of knowledge of religion. While it may have been one thing to gather with his peers in a religious association, to openly teach religion to these youngsters was still a new concept to an Ireland so long dominated by Protestants. As for education, these youngsters were illiterate because they could not afford even the few pence required by the pay schools. Edmund opened the New Street school for these boys in a stable in 1802.

Faced with the complaints of neighbors about the kind of young people who would now frequent the neighborhood, Edmund gave clear notice of his intent. Even though it was not considered necessary or even advisable in northern Europe or America to educate the poor, he "felt confident with the blessing of God to be able to uplift them and raise them to the status of men."[13]

Educating to Justice

From this small beginning, numbers of pupils quickly grew. The numbers of Edmund's confreres did not increase as rapidly but

---

[12] Ibid., p. 31.
[13] M.C. Normoyle, *A Tree Is Planted*, 1976, p. 42.

he was still able to form a religious society based on the Presentation Sisters' rule to carry out the task he had set himself.

If this were all that could be reported to determine Edmund's perspective on his mission, it may be insufficient to warrant the title of liberator. But what commenced as a means of raising the standard of living of generations of poor in Waterford and beyond soon took a clearer, more precise direction as Edmund again and again came up against the restrictions of Protestant administrators. Under these conditions, the success of the schools became the very testimony that caused the Irish people of his time to give him great respect.

One example alone may illustrate the point. When School Board inspectors came to the schools to determine their adherence to the many stringent English regulations, Edmund's Brothers taught the pupils to use the necessary subterfuge to avoid further persecution. One of the ruses of those early times is recorded by a pupil in verse.

Stop the Clock

So stands the fact, so runs the rule,
That in this ancient Christian land
From every state-assisted school
The Christian emblem must be banned;
That here on Ireland's hallowed ground,
The school must bear with fine and loss
If Irish youths therein are found
To bow their heads and sign the cross.
All honor to the Brotherhood
Who loving Ireland's children well,
And zealous for their country's good,
Refused in bonds like these to dwell.[14]

---

[14] W. Mark McCarthy, *Edmund Ignatius Rice and the Christian Brothers* (Dublin: M.H. Gill, 1926), p. 350.

The tone of this work would seem adequate confirmation of the fervent nationalistic spirit and desire for freedom that must have typified Edmund and his Brothers. As other oppressed peoples have found, a small incident of resistance, such as continuing the hourly prayer undetected, can build confidence for further acts.

It may then be understandable why the founder of the Christian Brothers and Daniel O'Connell, the pre-eminent liberator of Ireland, were such good friends. The Brothers stood out against the National System of Education imposed by England for secular schools. As one biographer writes,

> They stood consistently, not only for absolute freedom to develop their own system on the lines that seemed good to them, and in harmony with Ireland's aspirations and traditions, but also for freedom to teach the youth of Ireland their duty to God, to themselves and to their native land.[15]

It was at this time, too, that Daniel O'Connell was running for election as the first Catholic parliamentarian since the beginning of the penal laws. He opened his campaign with 14 days of meetings demanding full emancipation. The biographer claims, "The Founder, the Brothers and the pupils took the liveliest interest in these meetings."[16]

Subsequently O'Connell won the seat of Clare and in 1829 succeeded in achieving the Catholic Emancipation of Ireland. O'Connell followed up the Brothers' support by attending the laying of the first stone at the initial foundation of the Brothers in Dublin. O'Connell himself later praised the event as a great day for Ireland.[17]

---

[15] Ibid., p. 353.
[16] Ibid., p. 267.
[17] Ibid., p. 269.

Another biographer claims that O'Connell was always sure of the Brothers' prayerful support; he was always pleased to see the Founder. Upon meeting once on the train, O'Connell called Edmund the patriarch of the Irish monks and proceeded to engage him in a conversation which ranged from the conditions of the country at the time to the coming National Education System. In time, O'Connell wrote his support for the Brothers' opposition to the National Education System and gave his assurances that, if it were in his power, it would not be enacted.[18]

Eulogies

The outpouring of nationalistic sentiment at the death of Edmund Rice is therefore consistent with this view of him. One writer attributed to him the majority of the advancement of the country in civil and religious freedom.[19] Another claimed that next to O'Connell he helped bring about the victory of 1829. "One schooled the people for the guidance of the other."[20]

Finally, from the eulogy with which this section commenced,

> O'Connell won for the people Liberty, years after Brother Rice started educating the people. Brother Rice gave the education which has taught them how to use that liberty.[21]

---

[18] The Christian Brothers, *History of the Institute*, Vol. I (Dublin: Bray Publishing Co.), no date.
[19] M.D. Normoyle, *Memoirs*, 1979, p. 362.
[20] Ibid., p. 363.
[21] Ibid., p. 127.

Chapter Four

EDMUND'S TEXTS

The texts written on the flyleaf of Edmund's Bible are a further clue to the way he perceived the mission he was undertaking. Just as the dimensions of Edmund's life that typified a solidarity with the oppressed have been unintentionally suppressed over time, so the full significance of the texts in his Bible has yet to be realized. Contrary to the view of most of his biographers, they do more than simply indicate the sections of the Bible that had reference to his daily work.[1] Such a view of them denies the element of conversion. But the texts are more than a determination of the period of conversion also.[2]

As would be expected, the interpretations of the texts by each biographer arise from the general theological and scriptural thought prevailing at the time of writing. Thus the focal point of the texts can be seen as "cupidity,"[3] or they can be seen to indicate a conversion from an Old Testament view of the injustices of usury to a New Testament attitude of charity.[4] All interpretations that conclude that

---

[1] M.C. Normoyle, *A Tree Is Planted*, 1976, p. 30.

[2] A.L. O'Toole, *A Spiritual Profile of Edmund Ignatius Rice*, Vol. II: *Rooted in Love* (Bristol: Burleigh Press, 1985), p. 82.

[3] Ibid.

[4] A.L. O'Toole, *A Spiritual Profile of Edmund Ignatius Rice*, Vol. I: *More Than Silver or Gold* (Bristol: Burleigh Press, 1984), p. 44.

Edmund would "transcend the ideal of mere justice, to arrive at a generous compassion for the poor" are therefore seen as reductionistic, limiting the breadth of Edmund's vision.[5]

This book contends that, in fact, all of the above are inadequate representations of the texts, of course from the perspective of more recent biblical scholarship. It is true, as far as is known, that this information was not available to Edmund. He had only the text itself on which to rely. But what makes the more recent readings a better approximation to Edmund's own thought, it may be argued, is the provision in these methods for taking account of the contextual clues the Bible itself provides. Edmund was an assiduous and close reader of the Scriptures we are told (a skill he handed on to his pupils)[6] and therefore had a better chance of appreciating the full flavor of the texts than have those who read only the isolated texts.[7] It will be seen that some of his biographers give the impression of his having read the texts this latter way.

It is reasonable to assume, given the social nature of the topic in these texts that Edmund applied their meaning to the social conditions of his own time, conditions of widespread poverty. His later actions are evidence of this. With this in mind, the method of exegesis pursued here is that which has provided the poor of South America and other Third World countries with the will and the hope to endure under the harshest conditions of oppression and injustice. The foregoing material on Edmund's life shows quite similar conditions existing for the Irish Catholic poor of Edmund's time.

In fact, some of the parallels between Edmund's social context and that of South America today are quite striking. As in much of South America, 18th century Ireland was largely Catholic, under the economic (and in the case of Ireland, also the political and military) domination of foreign powers, and being bled of its natural

---

[5] A.L. O'Toole, *A Spiritual Profile*, Vol. II, 1985, p. 82.

[6] The Christian Brothers, *History*, p. 55.

[7] A.L. O'Toole, *A Spiritual Profile*, Vol. II, 1985, p. 85.

resources. The people were consequently predominantly poor, illiterate and politically powerless. As in South America, the people awaited a leader (O'Connell) who would rally them and begin the process of empowerment. And as in South America also, political leadership alone was not enough to regain for them their full independence and freedom.

There is another reason for comparing Edmund's reading of the texts with readings of the texts that are possible today. The similarity between these readings hinges on the question of context. Literary context includes (a) the relationship of the text to the biblical context; (b) the reading of the text against the background of history, politics and economics of the original audience; and (c) the reading of the texts against the historical, social and economic context of the modern reader: the Christian Brothers and their fellow workers in the various fields of ministry throughout the world.

The following reading of these texts then situates them in the contexts of Edmund's time and of our own. The similarities between these times, particularly for the Church and its mission, have already been drawn.

It is expected that this re-reading may further illuminate Edmund's intentions in founding the ministry he did and may provide a richer appreciation of his mission by Edmund's followers today. This may occur at two levels: on the one hand, the texts reveal Edmund's understanding of his own vocation in a unique and very personal way; on the other, they are a legacy which can give to his followers today new theological insights, even if they were not all intended by Edmund himself.

Section 1
MATTERS OF INTERPRETATION

The method of the application of Scripture to life is always controversial. Extremely literal renditions of the text have led in the past to the manner of proof-texting which legitimates almost any application without reference either to context or to the original intentions of the author. The historical consequences of this method are evidence enough of the injudicious and unauthentic nature of this interpretive device.

More recently, historical-critical methods have introduced interpretations that provide greater faithfulness to the text by using the elements of form and literary criticism together with such scientific data as is provided by archaeology and the dating of texts. Aurel von Juchen argues that these methods may lead only to an idealist and individualist interpretation which in present circumstances is deemed wholly insufficient because of the enormous social problems of our day.[8] Furthermore, Norman Gottwald identifies two major concerns of today that are not answered by older critical methods and which have in turn spawned new methods of exegesis. One is the imaginative reality of the literary medium of the Bible and the other is the social dimension of the history that is background to the text.[9]

These new methods have given rise to the possibilities of new interpretations and applications of the texts of Scripture. Hermeneutics, the science of understanding events and interpreting them in written form, is providing Scripture with fresh relevance for our time. In particular, Christians and other committed groups in the Third World have provided new readings of Scripture by making

---

[8] Aurel von Juchen, "What a Pastor Expects from a Materialist Reading of the Bible" in *God of the Lowly: Socio-Historical Interpretations of the Bible*, edited by W. Schottroff and W. Stegemann (Maryknoll, NY: Orbis Books, 1984), p. 7.

[9] Norman Gottwald, *The Hebrew Bible: A Socio-Literary Introduction* (Philadelphia: Fortress Press, 1985), p. 22.

connections between their own reality and the socio-cultural experiences of the biblical communities. In this sense, the grass-roots experience of Christians is being reinforced by new forms of biblical scholarship. Such a hermeneutic has freshness and relevance and relies upon what Croatto calls a "surplus-of-meaning" in the text that is revealed by posing new questions to it.[10]

This study into Edmund's texts is essentially a hermeneutic since it takes his own experience and the decisions he made and compares them with a better understanding of the text to determine what meaning has not yet been uncovered or has been left implicit.

Socio-Literary and Historical Methods

Hermeneutics are made possible through the influence of the social sciences on exegesis. Gottwald speaks of a new "sociological exegesis" that situates a book or text in its proper social setting by taking into account the literary and historical relationships between the parts and the whole. It attempts to illuminate the text according to its explicit or implied social referents.[11]

Advantages of this method are obvious in the case of the Christians already mentioned as providing a new hermeneutic for their own context in such places as Latin America, particularly when socio-literary / historical methods reveal the liberating dimensions of many books of the Hebrew and Christian Scriptures. In the essay already quoted, von Juchen gives eight examples of what may be expected from what he terms a "materialist" reading of Scripture. All of them seek to differentiate between the materialist and the idealist perspective. Two examples are the question of the effect of the nomadic existence of the Israelite community on its

---

[10] Servetto Croatto, *Exodus: A Hermeneutics of Freedom* (Maryknoll, NY: Orbis Books, 1981), p. 3.

[11] Gottwald, *The Hebrew Bible*, 1985, p. 28.

perception of the God of this journey and the differentiation provided by a materialist reading of the reign of God as opposed to the reign of various kings mentioned in the Bible. He concludes by underlining the connection between past experiences of the religious community and present realities. The same theologian who searches out the "living context" of the text must also be concerned with the community in the contemporary world, he says.[12]

Hermeneutics based on socio-critical methods can be seen to be a cyclic process in which the new experience of the community is tested against the experience of the community in its formative event (e.g., the Exodus, Jesus' death), using the skills of the socio-critical exegete. From the new reading of Scripture that often emerges, a new interpretation of present realities can be made. Not only is consistency seen between the past and present reality, but there is recognition that the God of Israel's history and of Jesus' experience is at work in the people's world today.

Section 2

THE TEXTS — A NEW READING: APPLICATION OF SOCIO-CRITICAL METHODS

The Texts

The following are the texts Edmund wrote:

Exodus 22:25	Proverbs 28:8
Leviticus 25:35-36	Ezekiel 18:12-13
Deuteronomy 23:19	Ezekiel 18:31
Psalms 15:5	Nehemiah 5:11
Psalms 55:11-12	Matthew 5:42
Proverbs 22:16	Luke 6:35

---

[12] Juchen, *Materialist Reading*, 1984, p. 11.

Internal Order

It may be unusual to speak of a single hermeneutic for so many disparate texts as is the case here, but what this study seeks to demonstrate is that precisely this approach is possible because of the inherent order and relationship that exists among these texts. At the most obvious level, Edmund's biographers have already seen this in their assertion that the theme of the texts is usury and its evils and that the movement of the texts from Hebrew Scriptures to Christian represent a conversion process in Edmund himself.[13]

The proposed order and relationship are as follows:

> The first three texts (Exodus 22:25, Leviticus 25:35-36, and Deuteronomy 23:19) form the background and unifying vision for the texts as a whole, a kind of gestalt of the issue being considered.
>
> The remaining Hebrew texts (Old Testament) simply apply this vision in particular circumstances or are generally in concurrence with it.
>
> The Christian texts (New Testament) form an ideal closure to the reflection by transposing the Hebrew vision into Jesus' own thought and teaching. They are at the heart of what it is to be both Jew, especially in Israel, and Christian, in the most radical terms.

Thus, for the purposes of this study, the texts can be regrouped in the following manner:

Key Texts	*Reliant Texts*	*NT Applications*
Ex 22:25	Ps 14:5	Mt 5:42
Lv 25:35-36	Ps 54:11-12	Lk 6:35
Dt 23:19	Pr 22:16	
	Pr 28:8	
	Ezk 18:12-13	
	Ezk 18:31	
	Ne 5:11	

---
[13] O'Toole, Vol. II, 1985, p. 82.

Seen in this light, the texts go well beyond the topic under consideration, viz. usury, to consider their implication for the Judeo-Christian life, a life to be lived in justice and in love. It will be left to the texts themselves throughout the remainder of this work to enunciate this vision and to reveal an interpretation based on the hermeneutic already proposed.

The Torah Texts

It may be supposed that some interrelationship between the first three texts would be possible, given their location within the Torah. But what is found upon a contextual reading is that all three come from the codes which form the centerpiece of the construction of each book. Exodus 22:25 is within the code of the Covenant (C), Leviticus 25:35-36 occurs in the Holiness code (H), and Deuteronomy 23:19 is in the Deuteronomic code (D). There is significant similarity between these three codes, giving evidence that one built upon the other as each one emerged from the community's continued reflection on its Mosaic origins and the importance of the law in its life and worship.

The Exodus Community

In order to contextualize these three codes then, it is necessary to place them within the framework of the Exodus and the determinants that placed on the embryonic Israelite community. Socio-literary and historical critiques give important clues to the nature of this community and the significance the codes had for it.

The Exodus community is portrayed graphically as an oppressed community in the opening chapters of the book of Exodus. They are depicted as working under taskmasters to build the cities of Pithom and Rameses (1:11). Anderson gives historical validity to this picture by tentatively linking the construction under Rameses

II and other Pharaohs during the 14th and 13th centuries B.C. with the slavery of the marginalized or recently arrived and unstable peoples who were used to build the great cities. These people were "*Habiru*," driven perhaps by migrating Hyksos.[14] To maintain the oppression there was virtually a policy of genocide. "If it is a boy, kill him; if a girl, let her live" (1:16). When the midwives used subterfuge to obstruct this policy, the command was given to drown the Hebrew boys in the river (1:22).

A dominant theme in these early chapters is that in their suffering the Hebrews cried to their God for deliverance (2:23). The divine response is seen to occur in the leadership of Moses. He had survived the fate of male children through the artifice and assistance of Pharaoh's daughter, giving him obvious status with the Egyptians, but upon visiting his own countrymen and women, he had his consciousness raised by their plight. The attack of an Egyptian on a Hebrew slave is sufficient to draw him into the struggle on the side of his people.

The ensuing empowerment of the Hebrews and their bargaining for freedom are well known. With the eventual escape from slavery and oppression and the journey to a land of freedom, the book sets the formative event of the Hebrews in the context of subjugation and liberation. Every development from this time on in Israelite history would be set against this motif of slavery and freedom.

But if credence is given to Norman K. Gottwald's *The Tribes of Yahweh*, identification of Israel's formation in the exodus event is difficult to sustain. He would rather see the historical roots of Israel and the covenant and law traditions as arising in the early Canaanite period of Israel's history. Covenanting and law-giving were relatively undeveloped for the proto-Israelite group compared with those in the later confederation.[15]

---

[14] Bernard Anderson, *Understanding the Old Testament* (Englewood Cliffs, NJ: Prentice-Hall, 1986), p. 53 ff.

[15] Norman Gottwald, *The Tribes of Yahweh: A Sociology of the Religion of Liberated Israel, 1250-1050 BC* (Maryknoll, NY: Orbis Books, 1979), p. 36.

And, if this is the case, for our purposes, the rooting of the codes in the initial confederations in Canaan give an even more pointed "liberation" aspect to the material. Gottwald's thesis, as stated elsewhere, is that Israel developed culturally and religiously from the revolutionary convergence of various marginalized groups and tribes within the broad national status of Canaan. This alliance occurred over a long period of time as the rulers of the city-states extracted tribute and forced labor from peasants to support their own luxurious lifestyle. He explains that during the 14th and 13th centuries B.C. restive nomads, *habiru* or *'apiru* and other disaffected groups were drawn into alliances to ward off the attempts at control by the city-states. With the arrival of the exodus community, the religion of Yahweh provided the socio-religious framework to help form these peoples into an effecting revolutionary movement to expel the tributary mode of production from the highlands and substitute a system of free agriculture in a loose tribal setting.[16] (It may be important at this point to footnote these remarks with a definition of *'apiru*. Gottwald defines them as "social outsiders," often living on the margins such as in mountain retreats. It is considered the etymological origin of the term Hebrew.)

What is significant in this theory for our purposes is that the tribal Israelite community was formed precisely as an egalitarian and anti-hierarchical society. Against this background, much of the societal norms of the codes make good sense historically.

What both the exodus event itself and the emergence of Israel in the land of Canaan reinforce is that there were a number of experiences that established for the community that their culture was liberationist at its roots and with each new layer of this experience the exodus material took on greater import and was further reinterpreted in the ensuing biblical books.[17]

The egalitarian society which was the concrete norm for

---

[16] Gottwald, *The Hebrew Bible*, 1985, p. 273.
[17] G. Pixley, *On Exodus* (Maryknoll, NY: Orbis Books, 1987), p. xviii.

Israelite development forms an important backdrop to the texts chosen by Edmund Rice. Concern for the marginalized and the victims of oppression was obligatory in a society which had sprung from such oppressive beginnings. Israel's own experience speaks clearly through these texts.

Section 3

AN EXEGESIS OF THE TEXTS: COMBINING HISTORICAL-CRITICAL METHODS

The schema to be followed in the ensuing exegesis then is first a consideration of the exodus material to establish an understanding of the nature of usury and its contextual parameters; then a study of what further elements are added to this view by the other two Pentateuchal books; a review of the other Hebrew texts in Edmund's Bible; and finally, a study of the Christian Scriptures as they reflect this vision.

The three texts from the Torah are being treated as a unit here because of their occurrence in the three codes which show common origins in the book of the Covenant. Before further discussion it will be of benefit to quote the three texts in full, noting the similarities already obvious.

> If you lend money to any of my people, to any poor man among you, you must not play the usurer with him: you must not demand interest from him (Ex 22:25).
>
> If your brother who is living with you falls on evil days and is unable to support himself with you, you must support him as you would a stranger or a guest, and he must continue to live with you. Do not make him work for you, do not take interest from him; fear your God, and let your brother live with you. You are not to lend him

money at interest, or give him food to make a profit out of it (Lv 25:35-37).

You must not lend on interest to your brother, whether the loan be of money or food or anything else that may earn interest. You may demand interest on a loan to a foreigner, but you must not demand interest from your brother; so that Yahweh your God may bless you in all your giving in the land you are to enter and make your own (Dt 23:19-21).

The common concern here is usury, the charging of interest on loans. If it is accepted that the book of Exodus represents the oldest tradition, then there is a progression of thought through the three examples. What begins as concern for the welfare of all God's people becomes concern for the brother (women did not have the chance for such economic involvement), whether familial or communitarian. However, what saves these texts from a very narrow concern for blood relatives is the insertion in the Leviticus texts of the comparison with the situation of the stranger or the guest. This statement places the prohibition against usury within the dominant attitude of the codes and indeed the whole Torah. As will be seen, the fact that the Hebrews themselves had been *'apiru* in at least the broadest sense of the word, meant that the concern for the stranger is a constant theme of the codes. It is then noteworthy that the treatment of the brother in need here is to be measured against that to be given the stranger. This in some way offsets the narrower interpretation of the book of Deuteronomy.

Contextual Considerations

It has already been determined that these texts occur within the codes in each of the three books. This offers important shape and meaning to any interpretation of them. No doubt these codes began as oral proclamation but by the time of writing they had achieved a high degree of systemization. A comparison of the schema of each reinforces their common concerns.

Book of the Covenant

1. Cultic regulations (Ex 20:22-26)
2. Laws protecting property and human beings (Ex 21:12-22:17)
3. Social and cultic laws (Ex 22:18-23:9)
4. Calendar of festivals and sabbatical times (Ex 23:10-19)

Deuteronomic Law

1. Cultic regulations and festal calendar (Dt 12:2-16:17)
2. Laws dealing with institutions of justice and religion (Dt 16:18-20:22)
3. Miscellaneous laws (Dt 21:1-25:19)
4. Concluding rituals (Dt 26:1-19)

Holiness Code

1. Animal sacrifice and the priestly system (Lv 17:1-16)
2. Holiness including sexual relations and penalties (Lv 18, 19, 20)
3. Instructions to priests (Lv 21-22)
4. Sacred calendar and priestly laws (Lv 23:1-24:23)
5. The sabbatical and jubilee years (Lv 25)
6. Appendix on religious observance (Lv 27:1-34)[18]

Some similarities are obvious at this level. The concerns with cult, sacred times and duties offer some intimations of the contents. But there is much more agreement between the codes when one considers the various proscriptions individually. Dale Patrick claims

---

[18] Cf. Dale Patrick, *Old Testament Law* (Atlanta: John Knox Press, 1985), pp. 66, 104, 155 and *The New Oxford Annotated Bible* (New York: Oxford University Press, 1973).

direct dependence of the Deuteronomic code on the book of the covenant.[19] Certainly the numerous parallels between the two (at least 20 can be identified) suggest if not common authorship at least direct reliance. The holiness code represents a different emphasis with its core material arising outside the P tradition, though there are still many elements of the priestly code interpolated.

For the present purposes, it is adequate to reiterate that these codes are interrelated in significant ways and that taken together they form the sum of the tradition of law and cult that began orally and was written finally some time during or after the exile.

The Exodus Text on Usury

Occurring in the third section of the Book of the Covenant as shown above, moral commandments and duties, this text is part of the first of three subsections which may be delineated as follows:

    A.   Rights of the weak (22:21-27)
    B.   Religious duties (22:28-31)
    C.   Court process and duties of assistance (21:1-9)

It is easily seen that if the treatment of the marginalized is a primary concern of the codes, the section of the Book of the Covenant in which Exodus 22:25 occurs is central. The experience of the exodus and later communities has now issued in a concern for the stranger or resident alien who does not enjoy the full rights of citizenship. Equality before the law is a very practical matter. It must be guaranteed for those who are at risk. The people in this condition are enumerated here: the stranger (v. 21), the widow and the orphan (v. 22), the debtor (v. 24, 25), the pledger (v. 26). It has been said that the stranger was a constant concern of the law; so too

---

[19] Patrick, *Old Testament Law*, p. 97.

were the orphan and widow. The text on usury therefore occurs in a legal passage, significant for its concern for the poor.

Patrick says of this section that the laws protected the rights of the weak, exemplifying the fact that each person in the community was given inalienable rights by God. If the respect given the weakest member is used as a test for a community's legal system, what more can be said where God alone is the patron of the society's marginal persons?[20]

Usury

> If you lend money to any of my people, you must not demand interest (Ex 22:25).

By its very nature, usury, the act or practice of lending money at an exorbitant rate of interest, is an oppressive practice towards the poor. It is quite understandable that a society founded on equality would wish to outlaw the practice at least within its own borders. In simple terms what usury does is to inflate the price of money. The poor requiring these loans would already have been the subject of oppression in the first instance by the very fact of being in this predicament. Usury amounted to a second level of oppression in which a tantalizing way out was offered the victim, but at the cost of further indebtedness. Money could double or treble its value at the discretion of the creditor. Shakespeare's *The Merchant of Venice* attests to the grotesque nature of this vice and even seems to attribute some of the European rancor between Christian and Jew to this practice by both parties.

The Scripture scholar, E. Neufeld, has made a number of studies of the texts on usury in the Old Testament, mostly from the perspective of the practical details of the interest charged. In his

---

[20] Ibid., p. 26.

commentary on the text in Nehemiah 5:11, one of Edmund's texts, he makes a point of the degree of oppression that may have been involved here. The moneylender had a free hand in ancient Israel to determine the rate, leaving the debtor entirely at his mercy. Such a rate fixed by usage was bound to be high. Evidence of this exists in the fact that there is constant sympathy in Scripture towards the debtor.[21]

But in an article that is even more revealing, Neufeld shows how the practice became more widespread and disruptive of society in the wealthier times that accompanied urbanization, particularly under the monarchy. He quotes Proverbs 22:7 which likens the borrower to a slave and says that this may not have been far from the truth. In the light of Edmund's extensive list of the texts against usury, it is worth noting the extent of Neufeld's commentary. He claims that the moneylender was condemned by Israelite society and that his increase of wealth was regarded as the result of exploitation of the poor. Biblical laws concerning the debtor regard him as the victim of misfortune who was not to be treated oppressively. The taking of interest was regarded as unjust profit. It was seen to be as bad as bribery. In ancient Israel, as elsewhere, creditors comprised a social class. Lending money helped them to keep the economically inferior borrowers in a state of subordination.[22]

The key elements of this understanding of usury in the Hebrew Scriptures for the appreciation of Edmund's texts are both the oppressive nature of the practice and the class distinctions it brought about. What Neufeld's work indicates for this study is that these views of usury are so pervasive in the texts that Edmund could hardly have failed to appreciate them, once his consciousness of the evils of the practice by his own social class became apparent to him.

---

[21] Edward Neufeld, "The Rate of Interest and Nehemiah 5:11," in *Jewish Quarterly Review*, Vol. 44, Jan., 1954, p. 197.

[22] Edward Neufeld, *The Emergence of a Royal-Urban Society in Ancient Israel*, pp. 46, 47.

Edmund's Texts

Essentially as a result of these texts, usury was strongly condemned not only in Judaism but also in early Christian practice. How much Edmund Rice knew of this is unclear because the prohibition had long since lapsed by the 18th and 19th centuries. In fact, it may be considered extraordinary that Edmund, on his own undertaking, reverted to a view of economic justice that had long been in disuse and was widely contravened in his own Irish and wider European society at the time.[23]

Yet usury remains the subject of much controversy. In a most significant condemnation of the practice, Richard Kelly Hoskins advances the theory that it was an essential ingredient in many wars and offers the insight that the Third World debt crisis is basically a case of international usury.[24] To highlight the implication of the practice he gives the homely example of a Babylonian lender giving a debtor 10 talents and asking 11 in return. His land, livestock, even his wife and children serve as collateral. In those days there was little money in circulation. When the 10 are returned he has only sheep and pigs to pay. But money was asked.[25] Since society today is basically a global entity Hoskin's treatment is worthy of note. Where money is borrowed on these terms internationally, the effect will be the same as that for the Babylonian debtor. Some estimate that the South American debt has already been paid 14 times over and yet there is still more owing. The United States of America, the largest debtor nation in the world, is ironically likewise held hostage to fluctuating interest rates which threaten its very status as a world leader in the coming century. And we know that several European countries find themselves in an equally precarious economic situation, with Japan having its own problems too.

The practice that Edmund saw to be so oppressive through his

---

[23] *The Catholic Encyclopedia*, Vol. 15 (New York: Encyclopedia Press, Inc., 1913), p. 235.

[24] R. Hoskins, *War Cycles-Peace Cycles* (Virginia: The Virginia Publishing Co., 1985), p. 76.

[25] Ibid, p. 1.

own experience and the reading of Scripture now has international implications. Debtor nations now find themselves in much the same position as the poor of Israel. The international banking system continues to offer a way out of total bankruptcy, but at a price. And as has been shown that price simply continues to increase. Little wonder that economists say that these debts can never be repaid. The Exodus condemnation of usury within the Israelite community could well be applied to the international community in our times.

Widows and Orphans

Before proceeding, it is well to focus momentarily on the text regarding widows and orphans which precedes the usury text. The biblical context of the text is significant. Many times in the Pentateuch (and other places as well) the Scriptures align widows and orphans with the stranger. The clearest example apart from this one occurs in Deuteronomy 24:20. "Let anything left be for the stranger, the orphan and the widow."

Given what has been said on the status of the stranger in Israel itself, it is important that the other symbols of oppression and suffering should be the orphan and the widow. While the stranger is sometimes mentioned alone in Scripture, rarely is the grouping of "widows and orphans" divided. The common cause of their indigence seems to have been appreciated. Patrick says that they were vulnerable because they had no adult male to defend their interests and provide a living for them. It was therefore up to the extended family and the community at large to defend their rights and take care of them.[26]

It may well be possible that Edmund's concern for the widows and single women of his day as well as his outreach to the children of the streets resulted from the consciousness-raising of these

---

[26] Patrick, *Law*, 1985, p. 86.

passages on the rights of the weak. In seeing the injustice of usury and its effects on those who would suffer most, he began to redress the balance of forces against them.

Conclusions on the Exodus Text

The section of the Book of the Covenant that has been considered closes as it opened with a reference to the experience of the *'apiru* of being strangers or aliens in the land. Exodus 23:9 reaffirms: "You must not oppress the stranger; you know how a stranger feels, for you lived as strangers in the land of Egypt." The laws on the rights of the weak are set within Israel's own experience of being outsiders.

One final comment on the Book of the Covenant as a paradigm for the other laws of the Hebrew Scriptures should be made. Following immediately upon the section just considered are the laws on sabbatical times and the festival calendar. It will be shown that this section also influences the interpretation of the usury laws. It is more explicit in the other codes, but here the very fact that they frame the rights of the weak is influence enough. It has been said that a striking feature of the fallow year and the Sabbath laws is their proximity to the laws protecting the rights of the weak (Ex 22:21-27; 23:9), suggesting that social concerns were an integral part of the evolution of Israelite cultic practice and theology.[27]

Leviticus and Deuteronomy

The Book of Deuteronomy is so close to the original treatment of the laws in Exodus that there is little benefit to be gained by a reiteration of the exegesis. The noteworthy element of the usury law

---
[27] Ibid., p. 92.

here is that it applies unfortunately only to Israelites and that foreigners are still permitted to enter such contracts. Here the insistence on the status of the stranger given in Exodus is overlooked though the law does occur within a group of miscellaneous laws emphasizing protection of the weak.

Of greater significance for our purposes is the text in the holiness code in the book of Leviticus. The code takes its name from the insistence to "Be holy, for I, Yahweh your God, am holy" (Lv 19:2). This holiness, however, is not to be understood in terms more commonly used in modern times. W.A. Turner identifies the holiness intended here, not as a giving up of some part of life, but as a submission to the superior member of the covenant in a covenant treaty.[28]

Holiness

There is the sense here of the reign of God in the lives of the people. Justice is the ordering of life so that all may live (cf. Lv 19:9, 10). To this God, all were strangers and have become community only by God's graciousness. This must be remembered in dealings with other strangers. The comments made above regarding the social nature of theology in Israel underline the fact that holiness entails justice for these people.

The code of holiness best exemplifies this theme in the books of the Pentateuch. It has the appearance of a development from the Exodus notion of the legal implications of the one God. "I am Yahweh your God" (Lv 20:1, 2). But in the holiness code, God is one in the sense of whole. "Be holy, for I, Yahweh your God, am holy" (19:2). This theme is reiterated again and again through the code, so that the conclusion must be that one is to be just because of

---

[28] W. Turner, *Leviticus*, *Collegeville Bible Commentary* (Collegeville, MN: Liturgical Press, 1985), p. 58.

the order and wholeness that it implies. The covenant is seen to be based on the wholeness of the superior partner. All of life can now be lived with this view. Israel's community is to reflect this wholeness in the order, equality and particularly the concern for the weak that it implies for relationships.

Edmund's Texts

The stranger and the poor are again cause for concern since they too have a right to the fullness of life (Lv 19:10). Therefore, when the code turns to the concept of a Jubilee Year as well as the Sabbatical Year (a development from the Book of the Covenant), it is most concerned for the status of the poor and marginalized. The Jubilee Year is instituted for every 15th year so that the people may "proclaim the liberation of all the inhabitants of the land" (25:10). Just as the Sabbatical Year was designed to rest the land, so the Jubilee Year is to rest the people and to restore all things to their original order. The people must return to their clans; the land is to lie fallow. "So you shall be secure in your possession of the land. The land will give its fruit, and you will eat your fill and live in security" (25:18-19).

Among the benefits of the Jubilee are to be the recognition of Yahweh as King (Lv 25:23), the redistribution of wealth (25:67), the gathering of families (25:10), the resting of the land (25:24), the enjoyment of liberty (25:10, 54), the fruitfulness of the land (25:19), the cancellation of debts (26:36, 37), and the lifting up of the poor (25:25, 35, 39, 47, 48). As Turner describes it, everyone and everything is to be whole in a life of wholeness (holiness).[29]

An interesting note is added in the text to the concept of land use already practiced. In Leviticus 25:23, God is seen as the owner of the land and all others are strangers and aliens who have become

---

[29] Ibid., p. 57.

tenants. This gives new import to the texts on the treatment of strangers since, if all are this way in respect to the land, the source of wealth, no one has a right to treat any other any more as an outsider. Wealth must be distributed, according to this logic. It may now be seen that the text chosen by Edmund Rice from this book (25:35-36) is contextually as significant as that in the Book of Exodus. The emphasis there on the equality and human dignity of all as cause for the prohibition of usury is extended here to the need to cancel all debts so that right order (wholeness) may return and that the oppression of the poor may cease. There is considerable hope in this law for the debtor, though he or she may wait a lifetime to realize it.

Usury in Leviticus

> If your brother who is living with you falls on evil days and is unable to support himself with you, you must support him as you would a stranger or a guest, and he must continue to live with you. Do not make him work for you, do not take interest from him; fear your God and let your brother live with you. You are not to lend him money at interest, or give him food to make a profit out of it. I am Yahweh your God who brought you out of the land of Egypt... (Lv 25:35-38).

The extension of the text beyond the verses quoted by Edmund situates them in the form in which he would have read them. In this form, all the important themes that have already been stressed from the covenant and holiness codes are reiterated. After reading these verses Edmund may well have felt he had already heard clearly what was being said, viz. that according to the "law" of the stranger or the guest (the *'apiru*), a member of the same community must not be charged interest since this is to make a profit from him. All that a person possesses has been given by God; it therefore must be shared. The principle is that it was God who liberated the bonded Israelites and they must remember this in regard to the oppressive practice of usury.

Patrick claims that the case here is that of a man who has sold his inheritance and has effectively become an alien. The law encourages the endowed members of his family to help him maintain solvency.[30] That justice and love are combined in the attitude to this insolvent is not uncharacteristic of the entire holiness code. The commandment to love the alien is a feature of the book. It occurs first in Leviticus 19:18 and is repeated in the second half of chapter 19 (33-34) and as such is a strong statement of the concern that must be had for the stranger. Jesus' ordering of the first two commandments and his extension of the love commandment to the "enemy" originate with this expression.

The commandment of love is the New Testament embodiment of what Patrick calls the "unwritten law" of the Torah. Many of the laws of the ancient Near East were orally transmitted for years before being written. Patrick claims that in the time of the formation of Israelite law, it was the sense of justice and right shared by the legal community and sharpened by the judges that formed the body of this unwritten law.[31]

At the heart of this unwritten law, therefore I suggest, is the commandment of love. Justice finds its full flowering in the law of love, especially love of the alien. It is Jesus' statement of the law as love that reveals the New Testament's links to the unwritten law. Jesus reaffirms the heart of the unwritten Torah.[32]

The point of this analysis of the Leviticus text for Edmund's vision is that the biographers who have claimed that the texts merely show a progression from an Old Testament understanding of the

---

[30] Patrick, *Law*, 1985, p. 184.

[31] Ibid., p. 189.

[32] Ibid., p. 208.

requirements of justice in regard to usury to one of love in the New Testament do grave disservice to the texts. The tension between justice and love is present from the first formulation of the laws and, as will be shown, the Christian understanding of debts is reliant on this section of the Torah. What the code of holiness text brings to the reflection Edmund undertakes is the insistence that love of the alien requires practical demonstration in just treatment, particularly by not burdening the poor with loans at interest.

Remaining Hebrew Texts

The other Hebrew texts Edmund used are as follows:

(The man)... who stands by his pledge at any cost, does not ask interest on loans, and cannot be bribed to victimize the innocent. If one does all this, nothing can ever shake him (Ps 15:5).

Day and night shall iniquity surround it upon its walls; and in its midst thereof are labor and injustice. And usury and deceit have not departed from its streets (Ps 54:11-12: Douay version as used by Edmund).

Oppress the poor and you enrich him, give to the rich and you make him poor (Pr 22:16).

Those who increase their wealth by usury and interest amass it for someone else who will bestow it on the poor (Pr 28:8).

(The son)... who oppresses the poor and needy, steals, fails to return pledges, raises his eyes to idols, engages in filthy practices, charges usury on loans and takes interest, then this son shall certainly not live (Ezk 18:12-13).

Shake off all the sins you have committed against me, and make yourselves a new heart and a new spirit! Why are you so anxious to die, O house of Israel (Ezk 18:31).

> Remit them their fields, their vineyards, their olive groves and their houses forthwith, and remit the debt on the money, corn, wine, and oil which you have lent them (Ne 5:11).

These other texts quoted by Edmund continue the attitudes established by the Torah towards usury, virtually without exception. Most of them, such as the two from the Psalms, merely reiterate the condemnation of usury. In each case, of course, the context adds much to the picture that is emerging of the widespread concern in the Bible towards this oppressive practice. For example, Psalm 55 speaks of God as the protector of the wronged. One example of oppression given occurs in verses 11-15.

R.J. Clifford sees this psalm as a lament, a prayer for deliverance and punishment of the enemy, an appeal to God's sense of honor.[33]

It has already been shown that Proverbs takes up the Torah material, though the example used is only one of a number on the subject. Edmund includes two others.

The Ezekiel quotes (18:12-13; 18:31) bring out the element of personal responsibility in the matter of usury; it was probably unnecessary by this time to remind Edmund of that if he had read with any care the preceding passages.

The Nehemiah (5:11) text has also received comment already. One element that it adds to the discussion, however, is important. The action of Nehemiah in regard to creditors is an excellent illustration of the societal implications of the practice and of the structural dimensions of the problem. Contrasted with the greed of the noblemen is Nehemiah's own humanity in seeking and ensuring an end to usury. As one who himself had been a creditor (5:11) he may well have modelled the solution to the evil for Edmund. Every

---

[33] R. Clifford, *Psalms 1-72*, *Collegeville Bible Commentary* (Collegeville, MN: Liturgical Press, 1986), p. 60.

description of him is surprisingly similar to the practical, shrewd businessman that Edmund had become. Nehemiah is shown as one with great leadership qualities, firm and courageous but also using diplomacy and humanity towards the poor (Ne 5:1-19). A sensible and practical politician, he was also deeply religious. This was shown in doing the necessary practical matters to preserve the faith of his people.[34]

Edmund's own response was just as forthright and liberating as Nehemiah's though he found his own creative means, education, for ensuring the faith of his own people. But his response to the poor who were being affected by usury was thorough as was Nehemiah's. Nehemiah had been angered by the nobles and officials who were ruining their neighbors by exacting interest which could not be repaid. When a warning did not succeed he assembled the whole people against them.[35]

From the Hebrew Scriptures, then, a very precise picture emerges of the extent, nature, implications and societal effects of the practice of charging interest on loans. For one who had read all the contextual clues to this interpretation so far, is it not fair to expect that he had seen something of the ramifications of the practice in his own life?

Christian Texts

If the New Testament texts varied greatly from the interpretation given so far, the argument of this book would be questionable. But it is clear that there is much to be gained from this view of the texts in that both the Matthean and Lukan texts are virtually

---

[34] Celine Mangan, *1-2 Chronicles, Ezra, Nehemiah: A Biblical Theological Commentary*, ed. by C. Stuhlmueller and M. McNamara, Old Testament Message, Vol. 13 (Wilmington, DE: Michael Glazier, Inc., 1982), p. 177.

[35] Ibid., p. 188.

Christian uses of the Torah material. The full quotation of the texts again may be helpful.

> Give to the one who asks of you, and don't turn away from the one who wants to borrow from you (Mt 5:42). If you lend to those from whom you expect to receive, what kindness is there in you? Sinners also lend to sinners to get back equal amounts. Instead, love those who hate you, do good, and lend expecting nothing, and your reward will be great. You'll be sons of the Most High, because He's kind to the ungrateful and the evil (Lk 6:35).

It is understandable that Edmund's biographers may have seen these texts as an advance on the Hebrew prohibition on usury. However, after the foregoing discussion it becomes clear that precisely the same condemnations of loans at interest are at the basis of these texts. The first offers the solution of giving to those who want to borrow (presumably the same groups of debtors mentioned in the Hebrew Scriptures); no mention is made of interest.

Then the Lukan text says it explicitly, "lend expecting nothing." And this is to happen in the same context of love as occurs in Leviticus for almost the same reason. Under God all are equal.

In a chapter entitled "The Implications of the Jubilee," John Howard Yoder uses these very texts to show that Jesus proclaimed the inauguration of the Jubilee as depicted in the code of holiness in Leviticus. It was stated earlier in the study of those texts that the remission of debts and the liberation of slaves was a feature of the Jubilee (Lv 25). Yoder shows Jesus' concern for the situation of the debtor in his parables and in the Our Father. One solution was the freezing of credit. Yoder says that Jesus uses the section quoted here from Luke to suggest other means of solving the debtor's problem. He continues the text on from "lend expecting nothing" down to "give, and it will be given to you" (v. 38). Giving is seen as a solution.

Jesus speaks to the debtor. He adopts an evenhanded approach. Both creditor and debtor are to act justly. The creditor can expect something if he gives freely. Then in the text from Matthew, Jesus clarifies his proposal by referring to the solution of the Pharisee Hillel (grandfather of Gamaliel) who had suggested the *prosboul*.[36] This was a means of the creditor transferring to a court the right to collect the debt in his name when the Jubilee would have cancelled it. Jesus' society was quite familiar with the Jubilee arrangements and endorsed them.

But in reply to this escape of the remission, Jesus offers the behavior to be negotiated on the way to the court of the *prosboul*: "To the one who wants to go to law with you and take your tunic, give him your cloak as well. And whoever forces you to go one mile, go with him two..." (Mt 6:40-41). So the text on usury in Matthew occurs in the context of what the debtor should do if repayment is required in the Jubilee Year. The creditor, by the same standard, should give and allow others to borrow, again presumably as in Luke, without expecting anything in return (interest).

Yoder summarizes the section of his chapter relating to these verses by showing that along with the parables of the merciless servant and the unfaithful steward they confirm that Jesus is really instituting a Jubilee. As was seen in the Leviticus texts such a Jubilee would resolve social problems by abolishing debts and liberating debtors whose insolvency had reduced them to slavery. Jesus does not offer a choice: to enter the Kingdom is to accept a Jubilee.

In choosing these two key texts, Edmund was already attuned to their meaning from his reading of the Hebrew texts. He would have appreciated the significance of Jesus' Jubilee solution: the remission of all debts and the redistribution of wealth. Edmund acknowledged that these texts had reference for his own life.

---

[36] John Yoder, *The Politics of Jesus* (Grand Rapids, MI: William B. Eerdmans Publishing Co., 1972), p. 74.

THE HERMENEUTIC

For Edmund's Life

It has been said that Edmund was extremely familiar with Scripture. Having procured the Bible at age 29, he proceeded through his life to read it thoroughly.[37] It is reasonable to assume that because Edmund was known to read the Bible so fully, the texts he chose, no matter what their source, were most likely read in their full literary context. And if this were the case, it is difficult to believe that he would not have seen at least some of their implications articulated here. The historical conclusions of these pages may not have been available to him but they clearly enrich what is an obvious theme of the oppressive nature of usury.

Contrary to the biographer's interpretation of the texts referenced in the beginning of this chapter, Edmund would have seen far more than the private, internal and personal effects of usury. He would almost certainly have been made aware of the whole public, societal and systemic dimension of usury. While admitting that the provisions trade put Edmund and his colleagues in Waterford in a position to exercise great influence as moneylenders, the biographer O'Toole does not make the connections with the oppressive effects of usury that have emerged through this reading of the texts.[38] The most O'Toole concedes is that Edmund might have been tempted to prey upon his poorer brethren.[39] Therefore, when he says that the texts in the Hebrew Scriptures protest against the injustice of usury, O'Toole does not seem to make the links to the injustice for which Edmund and his Waterford colleagues may have been responsible. It remains to Edmund's credit that he saw it and was converted.

---

[37] A.L. O'Toole, *A Spiritual Profile of Edmund Ignatius Rice*, Vol. I, op. cit., p. 42.
[38] Ibid., p. 43.
[39] Ibid., p. 44.

Some ten years after procuring his Bible, Edmund was to begin the relinquishment of his entire wealth and to spend his fortune in the feeding, clothing and education of the street kids in his city. What moneys were not spent in this manner were given either for the upkeep of poor widows in the town or for the support of the sister congregation from which he developed the Christian Brothers' rule, viz., the Presentation Sisters. The starkly scriptural parallels with the Hebrew concerns for widows and orphans are all too evident.

What motivated Edmund to such extreme measures? If he understood the ramifications of the texts he had read to any degree, he could not but have been struck by the power that usury gave the wealthy over the poor, marginalized and alien groups within society. It was an economic measure that ensured the increasing wealth of the few at the expense of the poor. It not only kept the poor in their place; it actually made them poorer. Edmund had read Nehemiah's condemnation of and his conversion from usury. He had heard Jesus' statements on the redistribution of wealth that signified the Jubilee. Giving without expecting return was the metanoia that would create equality and Edmund saw himself in need of this change of heart. Only in this way could the holiness associated with the "law of the stranger" be achieved.

How radical a conversion this may have been is suggested by the way oppressors are usually perceived in such places as South America today. It is considered extremely unusual for one of the wealthy class to abandon his or her class privileges, let alone the person's entire wealth, and join the poor. Such conscientization is rare. Not only did Edmund forsake the goods he had amassed, he eventually went outside the city walls to be with the poor in their own surroundings. As Gustavo Gutierrez has said, "One is only with the poor when one has friends amongst them."[40]

Having seen that the God of the *'apiru*, the aliens and outsid-

---

[40] Gustavo Gutierrez, Summer Course, Maryknoll, NY, 1987.

ers, expected a society where the poor were treated as equals with dignity, Edmund willingly moved not only to join his oppressed brothers and sisters but also to liberate them from the tyranny that a lack of education imposed on them in his day. He did not stop at the gift of his money and goods. His talents were to be shared also.

For His Followers

Whatever the understanding of Edmund's charism may have been in the past was culturally bound in its own time and place. New times require new initiatives. In a time when the questions of justice are again the test of Judeo-Christian love, the pattern of reflection and response seen in Edmund's life is important to his followers. If the Brothers and those drawn to the charism of Edmund Rice seek to refound his mission and ministry, would they not do well to return to its source? The ability to see the oppressive nature of wealth, to realize that class distinctions inevitably arise from the unjust or inordinate acquisition of wealth, is an important insight to be gained from Edmund's life. The desire to live on equal terms with others may well have practical applications in the area of material wealth. Edmund in his day and age gave a most heroic example of relinquishment and of what today might be termed "solidarity with the poor."

Especially significant, in a time when both women and children are again strongly represented among the marginalized, is the means Edmund chose to redress the evils of this oppression: education. The shape of new ministries is there in Edmund's life. Their accomplishment may require only his creativity and total commitment.

Motivated by the holiness of the One God, in community with God's people, such work for justice would itself bring wholeness.

CONCLUSIONS

This work sought to offer a rationale for the refoundation of the ministry of the Christian Brothers and others to "street kids" in the charism of Edmund Rice by:

(a) demonstrating the need for it in our times, using social analysis;

(b) providing a re-reading of Edmund Rice's life to show how his stance for justice led him to his ministry to the street youth of his day;

(c) analyzing Edmund's own scriptural texts to get a better understanding of what motivated him in his mission, thus clarifying its meaning and extent.

We have shown that the phenomenon of street kids is a serious sign of the social injustice prevalent in our times, an injustice which has physical, moral and psychological as well as social implications. At the same time we have suggested that a new model of education could provide a suitable and timely intervention with long-term results provided that it was undertaken in cooperation with other agencies. We have also tried to demonstrate how such a ministry would be very much in accord with the type of ministry Edmund himself undertook since his motivation grew from an appreciation of the injustice prevalent in his own day and its effects on the children of his own society. What would evidently be required of his followers for this renewal is a conversion of the order that Edmund himself underwent.

Some specific conclusions can now be drawn for both the ministry and the mission of the Edmund Rice family.

Refounding a Ministry to Street Kids

The analysis of these pages has suggested that the education of the young people presently on the streets is due them in justice. Looking upon and treating the child as an object, a commodity to be bought and sold, can be reversed by the rebuilding of a community around them which begins to treat them as subjects, human beings with dignity and worthy of respect. In this task the educational dimension will have to involve the children themselves in a reflection on their predicament and on their relationship to society as a whole. It has been demonstrated over and over again that given this opportunity, these youngsters can see through their experience of community the importance for themselves and for society of their commitment to a new vision of the way things could and should be.

The Christian Brothers and all those who follow the charism of Edmund Rice have two particular strengths to bring to such a ministry. There is, first of all, the professional skills which are needed, particularly in the Third World manifestations of this problem. While Cussianovich may have the correct notion of what is possible for his street kids in Peru, he lacks the professional background himself, and so do many of his co-workers, for providing a sound and lasting ministry. There are situations like this throughout the Third World. Edmund Rice's followers could do much to alleviate the suffering of these young people and their families with a well-researched and professionally prepared outreach to them.

Secondly, the Brothers' tradition, from the time of Edmund, of caring for the "little ones" as an expression of their solidarity with the poor almost demands such a response to the ever growing waves of street kids. Here is a very fundamental level from which the

Edmund Rice foundation can begin to bring about the renewal of society so necessary to our times.

Towards a Reformulation of Mission

The investigation of Edmund's life and particularly of his scriptural texts strongly suggest that he had a clearer notion of the words "instruction unto justice" than do many of his followers today. What is required in order to recapture this perspective on mission, a perspective that holds rich possibilities for the Church of the late 20th, even 21st, century is a recapturing of the vision of justice that Edmund's reading of Scripture may well have given him. The meditation of his texts may more fully reveal this.

But whether this reflection on the past is helpful or not, there remains the facts of Edmund's life and work and the weight of the scriptural word which have been bequeathed to the Congregation and the world for the present. Seeing the needs, it is unlikely that Edmund's followers can avoid the implications that have been drawn in this book. The whole Church deserves to experience, through sharing it, the example set by Edmund as a wealthy merchant who relinquished everything for the sake of bringing God's reign, God's justice into the world.

In the current search for the spirituality and charism of Edmund Rice, and by extension of the Christian Brothers' Congregation, it is important that the lessons provided by the code of holiness in Leviticus be fully absorbed. It is a lesson that such people as Gandhi and Merton and Mother Teresa, as well as Edmund, learned well. There can be no division between the contemplation of God and the works of justice. The Spirit of God is alive in the history of peoples today to bring about a renewal of civilization through the acknowledgment that God's holiness and love is the model for all human interactions and that it is God's task we undertake in liberating creation from the forces of sin and evil.

THE CENTRE EDUCATION PROGRAMME

A Christian Brother Initiative in Non-Formal Education

Sociologists have identified the phenomenon, in cities around the world, of the creeping "urban fringe" which typically houses the poorer, more alienated residents rejected by the city center.[1] In two of these fringes in Australia, Sydney's western suburbs and Brisbane's southern suburbs, the Christian Brothers and their co-workers have established small, flexible, community-based units to respond to the needs of the poorer inhabitants. Most work is of the social welfare and community development models. However, in 1984, the Brothers' Provincial Chapter in Queensland delegated Brother Terry Kingston to investigate the possibility of an educational response to the increasing numbers of young people spending their days on the streets of Logan City, Brisbane's excised southern fringe. It was pointed out to him that, along with the five high schools of the area, there was another "school" of truants on the streets every day, some 1500 youngsters roaming the supermarkets to offset boredom and partaking in petty crime or, often enough, the more serious crimes of car theft, drug-trafficking or prostitution.

---

[1] R. Grundy, C. Kingston, K. Wing, "A Carpet Snake in Our Yard: Life on the Urban Fringe," in *National Outlook*, Vol. 12, No. 8 (Sydney: Outlook Media Group, Oct. 1990), p. 23.

Terry based his response on a first-hand appreciation of the underlying causes of truancy. The high rates of unemployment, of single parent families and families in government-assisted housing, and of youth homelessness in Logan City were consistent with the conditions conducive to "pedism," already discussed here. The causes of truancy were seen to reside in the poverty of families in Logan City as well as the failure, at times, of the education system to meet the special needs of young people in such a predicament. Terry described the truants he met as youngsters who had "dropped through the cracks in the system."

In 1985, the Brothers supported the beginnings of an educational outreach to these young people with the acquisition of a house that had been used, formerly, as a drop-in center for unemployed young people in the city. Happily, the center was situated opposite one of the major high schools and could liaise with its administration for the retention of children who were enrolled but had been truanting from the high school. The first participants in the program approached the place because it was already known to them as a center for playing pool and table-tennis when they were absent from school. The two or three new arrivals had been consistently truanting for some 15 months, were well known to the local police and considered by social workers and teachers to be among the hard core of chronic truants in Logan City.

Terry and his group of volunteer assistants, including lay workers and other religious, patiently won over the trust of these early new students. From playing games, they proceeded to contracting with the students to make up some hours of schooling each week with a view to eventual reentry to the system. After a two year trial, this aim was abandoned as unattainable and The Centre, as it had become known to the students, set about establishing its own curriculum and exit standards. By the end of 1988, there were some 16 students aged between 13 and 16 years enrolled in the three-bedroom house which still served as their school. Staff numbers had risen to four full-time and two part-time members and minimal funding had been attracted from both Catholic and Government sources. Most of the costs were borne by the Brothers' own schools in Queensland.

In 1989, The Centre gained educational recognition by the very State system whose shortcomings had generated it. Funding required its annexation to the local De La Salle Boystown, but for other purposes it remains independent. It also changed residence to an abandoned set of eight shops which provided much needed space and allowed enrollment to increase to the present 25. Future plans include an outreach to the sprawling edge of the urban fringe where truancy, youth homelessness and offending are just as rife as they were in Logan City when The Centre began. Today, the curriculum includes attention to literacy and numeracy which are obvious casualties of the long months away from schooling, as well as manual subjects, preparation in life-skills, computers and the use of community arts to help the young people articulate their experience and to inform the wider community of these injustices.

Many of The Centre's visitors have remarked that the place seems to capture the essence of what Edmund Rice was doing in his response to the street youth of his time. Perhaps the obvious lack of inhibition among The Centre's students, and the signs of their brushes with life on the streets, as seen in their language and dress, serve to recall Edmund's efforts to encourage civility among his own students. It is consoling, too, to see the numbers of lay volunteers (men and women) who have come to throw in their lot with the Brothers in this new ministry. Often at great personal sacrifice they are willing to forego remuneration in order to participate in a venture which allows direct contact with the poorer ones of our society.

A DISCUSSION GUIDE

The Needs[*]

1. Who are the marginalized of your locality? Are there alienated young people? Where do they congregate? What are their conditions? pursuits?
2. Why are they like this? Who are their parents and where are they? What is their socio-economic background? How does it compare with yours? How many come from single parent families? Are their mothers and/or fathers employed?
3. What are their ages? Should they be at school? How long since they were? Are they employed? Could they be?
4. How effective are your local schools? the police? welfare agencies? government bodies? (with respect to young people).
5. Who in your society is benefitting from the situation of these young people? Who benefits indirectly? Who are kept in employment by these young people?

Finally, what conclusions can you draw from this survey?

---

[*] This set of questions requires the reader/s to undertake a survey (either first-hand or anecdotal) of local needs. They might question local welfare groups or young people themselves.

Edmund's Life

1. How much of this story was new to you? What parts of it surprised you? What aspects had you not considered before?
2. How did the story leave you feeling about Edmund? about the Christian Brothers? about yourself?
3. What aspects of this short biography do you wish to study further? Why?
4. What is your attitude to the interpretation of Edmund given here? What parts of it would you wish to change? On what do you base this?
5. Does this biography have any significance for you in view of the needs survey already completed? In what way?

Scripture Texts

1. What do you see as the common elements in all these texts? What are the major discrepancies between them?
2. How important do you think these texts are for the Edmund Rice legacy? How important are they to you?
3. What insights have you gained by reading the texts in their context? Can you justify these ideas from the context? from other Scripture texts? from the source material?
4. What do your discoveries say to followers of Edmund Rice today?
5. Are there other passages of Scripture to which these considerations lead you? If so, are they in any way derived from or dependent on Edmund's texts?

Conclusion

How would you interpret the following passage for the followers of Edmund Rice today?

Those who instruct others to justice shall shine like the stars for all eternity (Dn 12:3).

BIBLIOGRAPHY

Agnelli, S., "Street Children: A Growing Urban Tragedy." *Report for the Independent Commission on International Humanitarian Issues*, London: Weidenfield and Nicolson, 1986.

Anderson, B., *Understanding the Old Testament*, Englewood Cliffs, NJ: Prentice Hall, 1986.

Barbe, D., *Grace and Power: Base Communities and Non-Violence in Brazil*, Maryknoll, NY: Orbis, 1987.

Burrows, W., *New Ministries: The Global Context*, Maryknoll, NY: Orbis, 1980.

Carty, J., *Ireland 1607-1782* and *Ireland 1783-1850*, Dublin: C.J. Fallon Ltd., 1958 and 1953.

Catholic Encyclopedia, The, Vol. 15, New York: Encyclopedia Press Inc., 1913.

Christian Brothers, The, *History of the Institute*, Vol. I, Dublin: Bray Publishing Co., no date.

Clifford, R., *Psalms 1-72, Collegeville Bible Commentary*, Collegeville, MN: Liturgical Press, 1986.

Coles, R., *Children in Crisis: A Study of Courage and Fear*, Boston: The Atlantic Monthly Press, 1967.

Coles R., *The Moral Life of Children*, Boston: The Atlantic Monthly Press, 1986.

Constitutions of the Christian Brothers, 1985, p. 47.

Croatto, S., *Exodus: A Hermeneutics of Freedom*, New York: Orbis Books, 1981.

Freire, P., *Pedagogy of the Oppressed*, New York: Herder and Herder, 1968.

Freire, P. and Shor, I., *A Pedagogy for Liberation: Dialogues on Transforming Education*, S. Hadley, MA: Bergin & Garvey Pubs., Inc., 1987.

Gottwald, N., *The Hebrew Bible: A Socio-Literary Introduction*, Philadelphia: Fortress Press, 1985.

Gottwald, N., *The Tribes of Yahweh: A Sociology of the Religion of Liberated Israel 1250-1050 BC*, Maryknoll, NY: Orbis Books, 1979.

Harrington, M., *The New American Poverty*, New York: Holt, Rinehart and Winston, 1984.

Holland, J. and Henriot, P., *Social Analysis: Linking Faith and Justice*, Maryknoll, NY: Orbis Books, 1983.

Hoskins, R., *War Cycles-Peace Cycles*, Virginia: The Virginia Publishing Co., 1985.

Lebacqz, K., *Six Theories of Justice*, Minneapolis: Augsburg Publishing House, 1986.

McCarthy, W.M., *Edmund Ignatius Rice and the Christian Brothers*, Dublin: M.H. Gill, 1926.

Mangan, C., *1-2 Chronicles, Ezra, Nehemiah: A Biblical-Theological Commentary*, Edited by C. Stuhlmueller and M. McNamara, Old Testament Message Vol. 13, Wilmington, DE: Michael Glazier, Inc., 1982.

Neal, M., *The Just Demands of the Poor*, New York: Paulist Press, 1986.

Neufeld, E., "The Rate of Interest and Nehemiah 5:11" in *Jewish Quarterly Review*, Vol. 44, Jan. 1954.

Neufeld, E., *The Emergence of a Royal-Urban Society in Ancient Israel.*

Normoyle, M.C., *A Tree Is Planted: The Life and Times of Edmund Rice* and *Memoirs of Edmund Rice*, both for private circulation, 1976 and 1979.

O'Toole, A.L., *A Spiritual Profile of Edmund Ignatius Rice*, Vol. I: *More Than Silver or Gold* and Vol. II: *Rooted in Love*, Bristol: Burleigh Press, 1984 and 1985.

Patrick D., *Old Testament Law*, Atlanta: John Knox Press, 1985.

Pixley, G., *On Exodus*, Maryknoll, NY: Orbis Books, 1987.

Rushe, D., *Edmund Rice: The Man and His Times*, Dublin: Gill and Macmillan, 1981.

Synod of Bishops, *Justice in the World*, Rome 1971 in *The Gospel of Peace and Justice*, Edited by Gremillion, Maryknoll, NY: Orbis Books, 1976.

Turner, W., *Leviticus* in *Collegeville Bible Commentary*, Collegeville, MN: Liturgical Press, 1985.

von Juchen, A., "What a Pastor Expects from a Materialist Reading of the Bible" in *God of the Lowly: Socio-Historical Interpretations of the Bible*, Edited by Schottroff, W. and Stegemann, W., Maryknoll, NY: Orbis Books, 1984.

Willis, P. *Learning to Labor: How Working Class Kids Get Working Class Jobs*, New York: Columbia University Press, 1977.

Yoder, J., *The Politics of Jesus*, Grand Rapids, MI: William B. Eerdmans Publishing Co., 1972.